Wired int Teaching Jewish Holidays

An Internet Companion

Scott Mandel

A.R.E. Publishing, Inc.
Denver, Colorado

Published by:
A.R.E. Publishing, Inc.
Denver, Colorado

Library of Congress Control Number: 2002117429
ISBN 0-86705-082-9

Printed in the United States of America
10   9   8   7   6   5   4   3   2   1

Dedication

This book is dedicated to my great-aunts Alice (may she rest in peace), Edith, and Jean, with whom I grew up in Cleveland. Holidays were always very special times in my extended family — at one point we had five generations celebrating together. My great-aunts, along with their sister, my grandmother, created their own special holiday dishes that I will never forget: chocolate pie and strawberry shortcake, mandel brot, homemade hot pickles, shoulder steak, farfel (but they always seemed to forget the mushrooms), chopped eggs, and chicken soup with ketchup (it's actually quite good!). As I wrote this holiday book, I remembered and cherished these unique women.

Acknowledgements

Once again, I want to give special thanks to my editor and friend, Steve Brodsky of A.R.E. Publishing, Inc. His expertise and guidance have been invaluable in bringing this book to fruition, and making the entire "Wired into . . . " series a reality.

I am also indebted to Melodie Bitter, Mimi Hiller, Ben Zion Kogen, and Robert Schuck, who reviewed the manuscript, tried out the web sites, and offered their excellent ideas, suggestions, and insights.

Finally, my sincere thanks go once again to all of the educators and programmers who have taken the time to post their educational accomplishments on the Internet. Through their commitment and energy, they have made the cyberworld an online Jewish educational utopia.

CONTENTS

INTRODUCTION

Mrs. Lieberman was planning her unit on Pesach. She was tired of doing the same things every year. The students had grown bored with the "model *Seder*" that never varied — even the shank bones were frozen and kept from year to year. Mrs. Lieberman's chief resource was *Teaching Jewish Holidays*[1], a book with many great ideas and teaching strategies. However, many of the creative activities suggested in the book required information or materials to which she did not have easy access.

Thinking creatively, Mrs. Lieberman turned to the Internet — the Ultimate Jewish Resource Center. There she was able to find new, interesting, and innovative curricular materials to supplement her holiday curriculum, and to help implement the many creative ideas found in *Teaching Jewish Holidays*. For example[2]:

Through pictures and information found at the **CNN – MAKING MATZAH A PASSOVER TRADITION** Internet site, Mrs. Lieberman was able to teach her students all of the steps in making *matzah*.

New, creative Dr. Suess-like versions of sections of the *Haggadah* were downloaded from **UNCLE ELI'S HAGGADAH** and used in the school's model *Seder*.

---

[1] Goodman, Robert. *Teaching Jewish Holidays: History, Values, and Activities* (Revised Edition) Denver, CO: A.R.E. Publishing Inc., 1997.

[2] All of the URLs for these sites can be found in the Pesach section of this book.

A list of the latest "Kosher for Pesach" foods was found on the **KOSHER FOR PASSOVER** web site and discussed in class.

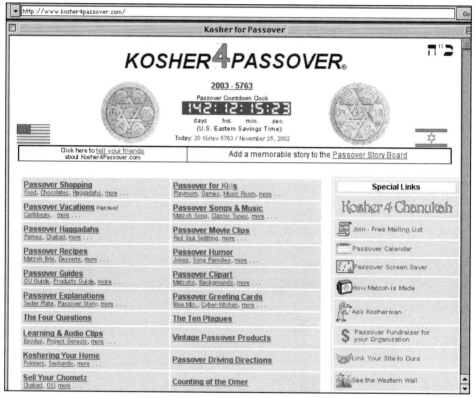

FIGURE 1

Since Mrs. Lieberman didn't have access to the Internet in her classroom, she created a Parent Pesach Newsletter to supplement her curriculum. The newsletter included the following sites for families to explore on their home computers:

Students and parents could learn all about the *Seder* plate at the **VIRTUAL SEDER PLATE** web site.

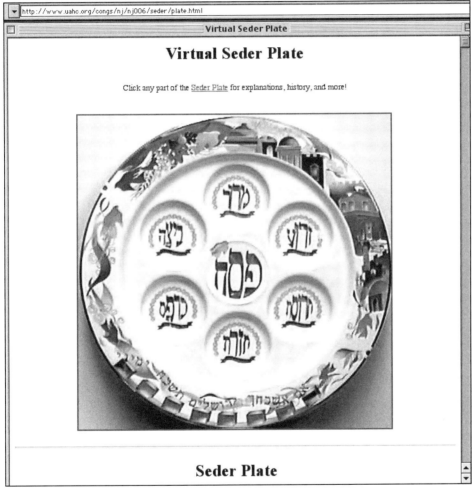

FIGURE 2

At the **JEWISH MUSIC HOME PAGE**, students could download and listen to examples of *Pesach* songs.

The Purpose of This Book

This book is designed to provide immediate Internet resources for many of the text study lessons and arts activities suggested in the book *Teaching Jewish Holidays*. However, the material included in this work extends beyond that book to any curriculum concerning the teaching of Jewish holidays. When you come across an item applicable to one of the holidays that you are teaching, or when you decide to incorporate a strategy from *Teaching Jewish Holidays*, you can simply access one of the URLs listed on these pages and find a wealth of supplementary material — text, photographs, drawings, maps, and detailed explanations of obscure or archaic terms. All that is required is a computer at home; school or student online access is not a prerequisite. For example, in the opening anecdote, Mrs. Lieberman could simply print a copy of the material on how to make *matzah* from her home computer and bring it into class. If she would like each student to have his/her own copy, she could duplicate the material on a school copy machine.

The process is both simple and extremely worthwhile. Curricular ideas that might not be attempted in class due to a lack of materials can now easily be integrated into your teaching on a regular basis. Following are some quick examples of how using the Internet resources listed in this book can immediately enrich your teaching, regardless of the holiday curriculum you are using.

HOLIDAY: SHABBAT
CATEGORY: Historical Ties
SUBJECT: Shtetl
EXPLANATION: Investigate how Shabbat was celebrated in the *shtetl*.

> **SITE:** ShtetLinks Page — Pilzno, Poland
> **URL:** www.shtetlinks.jewishgen.org/pilzno/pilzno.html
> **NOTES:** Lots of information about life in Pilzno, an excellent example of a *shtetl*. Be sure to read through the memoirs of its residents.

HOLIDAY: ROSH HASHANAH
CATEGORY: Ritual Objects
SUBJECT: Shofar
EXPLANATION: The *shofar* is a ram's horn blown on the High Holy Days.

> **SITE:** Shofar
> **URL:** www.uahcweb.org/ny/tinw/ReligiousLiving/
> ReligiousObjects/Shofar.htm
> **NOTES:** This site contains numerous pictures and explanations as well as the blessings connected with blowing the *shofar*. Also included are links to wav files[3] to listen to the *shofar*.

HOLIDAY: SIMCHAT TORAH
CATEGORY: Ritual Objects
SUBJECT: Rimmonim
EXPLANATION: These are the "crowns" on the Torah.

> **SITE:** Collections — Highlights
> **URL:** www.ncartmuseum.org/collections/highlights/judaic.shtml
> (see Figure 3, p. xiv)
> **NOTES:** This museum web site has a number of examples of *rimmonim* from around the world. Click on the link "Click here for more information" to view an enlarged picture.

---

[3] Wav files are music files that can be downloaded to your computer. The special software required to play them is typically installed as part of your computer's operating system — Windows Media Player on PCs and iTunes on newer Macintosh machines. If your system does not have this software, it is available free online from Microsoft (www.microsoft.com) or Apple (www.apple.com/itunes). Third party media players are also available for free, such as RealOne Player from RealNetworks (www.real.com).

HOLIDAY: YOM HAATZMA'UT
CATEGORY: Themes
SUBJECT: Chalutzim
EXPLANATION: The *Chalutzim* were the Jewish immigrants to Israel who began to arrive with the First Aliyah in 1882. They were largely responsible for transforming the semi-arid land into what it is today.

> **SITE:** Central Zionist Archives
> **URL:** www.wzo.org.il/cza
> **NOTES:** The archives site for the World Zionist Organization. Click on the "Exhibitions" link for a number of additional links to artifacts that display the work of the *Chalutzim*.

These are just a few examples of the ways in which you can quickly enhance your holiday curriculum through the use of supplemental resources found on the Internet.

FIGURE 3

How to Use This Book

The material in this book is meant to supplement your existing holiday curricula. This book does not provide teaching strategies or suggestions on how to teach holidays to your students; *Teaching Jewish Holidays* by Robert Goodman (and/or your school curriculum) provides various teaching ideas and directions for your classroom activities. Rather, this book provides you with Internet resources to enhance and extend the teaching strategies you select in order to fulfill the goals of your particular holiday curriculum.

This book, *Wired into Teaching Jewish Holidays,* is divided into 17 different holiday sections:

- Shabbat
- Rosh HaShanah
- Yom Kippur
- Sukkot/Hoshana Rabbah
- Shemini Atzeret/Simchat Torah
- Chanukah
- Tu B'Shevat
- Purim
- Pesach
- Yom HaShoah
- Yom HaZikaron
- Yom HaAtzma'ut
- Lag B'Omer
- Yom Yerushalayim
- Shavuot
- Tishah B'Av
- Rosh Chodesh

Please note that although this book contains well over 200 topical listings, not every term, item, or concept mentioned in *Teaching Jewish Holidays* or your own individual holiday curriculum can be found on the Internet. However, the world of cyberspace is constantly evolving, and by the time that you read this book, a web site may well have been established. Therefore, if there is something in *Teaching Jewish Holidays* that is not listed in these pages, refer to "What to Do If Something Can't Be Found Online," below, for tips on how to discover quickly if a new online resource exists.

As you plan for teaching a specific holiday, refer to the appropriate section to identify potential supplemental materials. For example, in planning for a unit on the holiday of Sukkot, you might look for an example of each of the individual four species. Then, simply type in the URL that is provided and go to that online resource, making note of any special instructions about locating material on that site. Then, you can:

> Print out the pages that you want to use in their entirety[4]. Bring to class one copy to use as a teacher resource, or make duplicates for your students.

> Select certain portions of the material, such as a picture, that you wish to use. Copy and paste the section onto a blank page in your word processing program, and then print out that page. This choice also allows you to add descriptions or titles if you choose. Bring in one copy as a teacher resource, or make duplicate copies for your students.

> Bookmark the site so that you can return to it easily in the future. For instructions on bookmarking, refer to Appendix B on page 173.

What to Do If Something Can't Be Found Online

The Internet is rapidly evolving, and millions of new pages are added every week. Internet sites come and go quickly, usually without advance notice. Therefore, some of the sites listed in this book may not exist when you attempt to use them, or may be temporarily unavailable. If that occurs, do not panic; rather, follow these simple steps:

---

[4] Please research the copyright laws in your state. Most states have what is referred to as a Fair Use policy, which allows teachers to print material from the Internet for classroom distribution only, as is recommended in this book.

1. Check carefully the text you typed to make sure that it matches *exactly* the address given in this book. If one letter is incorrect or a dot or slash is in the wrong place, your browser will be unable to find the requested page. Also note that URLs are case sensitive, meaning that typing the proper capital and lower case letters is critical.

2. Wait a day or two. Internet sites "go down" for a variety of reasons, including weather conditions that affect telephone data lines. For example, a storm in Atlanta can affect Internet access in Los Angeles. Internet data travels all over the world via routes that are hard to fathom.

Site maintenance may be in progress, which may cause the site to go off-line for a few days while being updated or for equipment upgrades.

A number of Orthodox sites shut down on Shabbat and Jewish holidays. (Note that because the Internet is an international community, it may officially be a holiday in some locations hours before or after other places).

3. Attempt to access other pages of the site, working upward through the hierarchy of pages until you reach the root page. For example, when searching for information about Maimonides, you might type

www.us-israel.org/jsource/biography/Maimonides.html

Perhaps you find that page unavailable. Try retyping the address, leaving off the text at the far right of the address, including the last slash:

www.us-israel.org/jsource/biography

Then push "enter" or "return." In this case, your browser will bring up a graphic free page showing the index of biography pages available. Scroll down and click on "Maimonides.html" to find the page you wish to view.

You can move up one more level by typing

www.us-israel.org/jsource

You will then find yourself in the "lobby" of the Jewish Virtual Library, with dozens of links to material on History, Women, the Holocaust, Travel, Politics, and much more. Finally, you can move up one more level and access the "root" page of the site

www.us-israel.org

This is the home page of the Jewish Virtual Library. This trick can also be useful in determining something about the organization that sponsors a particular site. In this case, by clicking "About Us," you can learn about the American-Israeli Cooperative Enterprise. The great thing about the Internet is that in the course of browsing and exploring various links, you just might find something even more valuable or interesting than the original document you were seeking.

4. Do a meta-search of the topic, the name of the item, person, or organization. Use a meta-search engine such as METACRAWLER (www.metacrawler.com) to ascertain if the URL has been changed, or if an alternate site now exists. Simply type in the name of the item, person, or organization that you wish to find in the search box, select the "phrase" button (if the search term contains more than one word), and click on "search" or hit the "return" button on your keyboard[5]. You will be provided with a list of links and descriptions that you can visit to find material that suits your needs.

5. Do a full search using general search sites, along with secular educational and Jewish educational sites. This is a more lengthy, although valuable, process and is well beyond the scope of this book. Detailed information on how to conduct a full Internet search for curricular materials can be found in *Wired into Judaism: The Internet and Jewish Education*[6]. That book provides you with a step-by-step description of how you can locate easily and systematically virtually

---

[5] Some computers have an "Enter" rather than a "Return" key. The terms are synonymous and refer to the same key on the keyboard.

[6] Mandel, Scott. *Wired into Judaism: The Internet and Jewish Education*. Denver, CO: A.R.E. Publishing, Inc., 1999.

any curricular resource on the Internet. The book also contains two very important sections that are both valuable and relevant to any search for Internet materials that you may undertake:

A section entitled "How to Evaluate Internet Sites" provides a form you can use to assess the utility of sites, taking into account their pedagogical outlook (i.e., Orthodox/Reform, Israeli right wing/left wing, Jewish/Christian/secular), and the educational value of the material that the site contains.

A section entitled "Accessing Hebrew Web Pages," which walks you through the steps to configure your computer properly so that you can display pages that are written in Hebrew.

Additional Tips

Here are a number of potential areas of concern that you may have as you explore the Internet sites listed in this book:

Commercial Sites: Some of the listed sites are commercial in nature, in particular those that contain ritual objects. However, these sites often provide photographs or drawings that can be valuable in the classroom. To copy a picture, right-click on the image, select "copy," then paste the image into a new word processing or page layout document. Add any captions or descriptive text and print. Of course, you can always simply print the entire page directly from the site and bring it to your students.

Non-Jewish sites: Some of the best material on the study of biblical issues can be located at non-Jewish sites. Since you are searching for teacher resources versus student-read material, this should not present a significant problem. Simply edit the material as needed. For an explanation of the importance and benefit of using non-Jewish sites in your Internet searches, along with a form on how to evaluate these sites, see *Wired into Judaism* by Scott Mandel, pp. 37-39, pp. 139-141.

Organizational/Judaism sites: The URLs to these sites typically direct you to the organization's main (or "home") page. You may have to explore the site a bit to locate the exact material that you require. If you are unable to find the material you need, an e-mail address is often posted, allowing you to contact the organization with any questions you may still have.

Small pictures/graphics: Most of the pictures of objects and art are rather small on the screen. These are called "thumbnail" graphics. Often, when you move your cursor over the picture, it will turn into a hand with a finger pointing. This means that you can click on the picture to see an enlarged view. You can then print the enlarged picture for your students, or copy and paste it into a new word processing or page layout document.

Spelling Differences: Unfortunately, there is no "standard" English spelling for transliterated Hebrew, and Internet sites use widely differing spellings. For example, the Purim noisemaker can be found on the Internet with at least three different spellings: "gragger," "gregger," and "grogger." A search using any of these spellings could yield different results. Be also aware of differences in pronunciations (and subsequent transliterations) of Sephardic and Ashkenazic terms[7].

Therefore, in order to make your online searches go more smoothly, all web site titles are presented using the transliteration provided by that site. Be aware that this may cause some confusion, so use the *exact* spelling provided in this book for titles of sites.

For a more detailed explanation of this problem, see "Spelling Does Count," page 77, in *Wired into Judaism*.

Now, let us begin to explore the hundreds of outstanding Internet sites that will be valuable in your teaching of and celebrating the Jewish Holidays.

---

[7] For some helpful advice on "creative spelling" when searching online, see the file on this subject on Mimi's Cyber-Kitchen (www.cyber-kitch.com/index/advice.htm).

Internet Resources by Holiday

The following material parallels the suggested activities and teaching strategies for each holiday listed in *Teaching Jewish Holidays*. If you are using that resource, visit the suggested URLs to find supplemental material that will enhance your students' study of any particular holiday. If you are not using *Teaching Jewish Holidays*, but rather are incorporating your own school's holiday curriculum, then use the resources listed for each of the holidays below to find valuable supplemental material to present to your students.

The sites listed below are just a starting place — there is much more material available in cyberspace than could possibly be listed here. As you browse the Internet, don't be afraid to follow the links you find — they will take you to many additional interesting and valuable sites.

The listing for each holiday contains the following information:

- **CATEGORY** – The overall category of the listing
- **SUBJECT** – The specific topic area covered by the listing
- **EXPLANATION** – An explanation of how the material on the site directly relates to this particular holiday.
- **SITES** – One or more sites that provide good curricular information relating to this subject. Each of these listings include:
  - The **TITLE** of the site
  - The **URL** of the site
  - **NOTES** about the site to help direct you to pertinent material quickly, or factors to take into consideration as you use the site

Updated active links to all the sites listed in the following section can be found on the A.R.E. Publishing, Inc., web site at www.arepublish.com/wired.html.

Shabbat

CATEGORY: Arts
SUBJECT: Fiddler on the Roof
EXPLANATION: This play and movie contain tremendous examples of preparing for and celebrating Shabbat. Especially note "Sabbath Prayer."

> **SITE:** Fiddler on the Roof
> **URL:** members.aol.com/Avena/fiddler.html
> **NOTES:** This site includes a summary of the musical taken from the actual show program.

> **SITE:** Fiddler on the Roof Lyrics
> **URL:** www.geocities.com/Broadway/Balcony/5705/Fiddler.html
> **NOTES:** Scroll down for a copy of the lyrics to the song "Sabbath Prayer."

CATEGORY: Arts
SUBJECT: Shabbat Music
EXPLANATION: There are many different types of Shabbat music.

> **SITE:** The Jewish Music Home Page
> **URL:** www.jewishmusic.com
> **NOTES:** Click on the link "Audio Library," then "Sabbath." You can listen to a number of selections of Shabbat music using Real Audio.

> **SITE:** Shabbat-Friday Night Zemirot in Audio
> **URL:** www.campsci.com/rvideo/friday_night.htm
> **NOTES:** A number of audio files of Shabbat *zemirot* for listening.

CATEGORY: Arts
SUBJECT: Shabbat-Themed Art
EXPLANATION: There are numerous artistic depictions of Shabbat.

SITE: World Wide Arts Resource
URL: wwar.com
NOTES: Type the word "Sabbath" in the "Indepth Arts Search" box. You will be given numerous links to search through to find appropriate sites.

CATEGORY: Food
SUBJECT: Challah
EXPLANATION: *Challah* is the special braided loaf of bread for Shabbat dinner.

SITE: Challah
URL: biblicalholidays.com/Sabbath/challah.htm
NOTES: Includes a detailed recipe for making *challah*. Note that this page is part of a Christian site, with a link to a "Messiah" reference on the bottom. The page however, is excellent.

SITE: Shabbat Customs and Traditions
URL: www.bus.ualberta.ca/yreshef/shabbat/shabcustoms.html
NOTES: Click on the picture of the *challah* for an article and pictures of the ceremony of eating *challah* on Shabbat.

CATEGORY: Food
SUBJECT: Cholent
EXPLANATION: *Cholent* is a Shabbat stew prepared on Friday, left to cook overnight, and eaten for Shabbat afternoon lunch.

SITE: Cambridge University Cholent Society
URL: www.cam.ac.uk/societies/cujs/cholent (see Figure 1-1, opposite)
NOTES: Everything you might possibly want to know about *cholent*, including recipes.

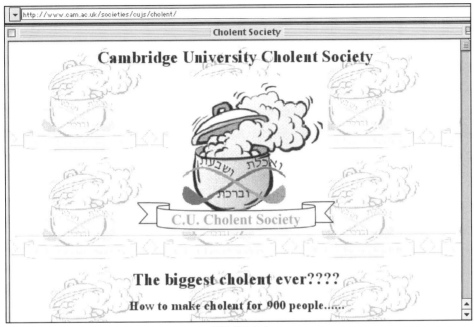

FIGURE 1-1

SITE: Jewish Food Mailing List Archives
URL: jewishfood-list.com
NOTES: Click on the "Recipes" link in the left column, then scroll down and click "Shabbat" for over 50 recipes.

CATEGORY: Food
SUBJECT: Shabbat Food
EXPLANATION: These sites provide recipes for various Shabbat foods.

SITE: Jewish Food Mailing List Archives
URL: jewishfood-list.com
NOTES: Click on the "Recipes" link and select from the choices provided.

SITE: Mimi's Cyber-Kitchen
URL: www.cyber-kitchen.com/rfcj
NOTES: Click on "Mimi's Recipes," then scroll through to select dishes that you would like to try.

CATEGORY: Historical Ties
SUBJECT: Manna
EXPLANATION: It is traditional to have two loaves of *challah* on Shabbat, symbolizing the double portion of manna that the Israelites received in the desert on Friday for Shabbat.

SITE: The Challah Connection — Facts
URL: www.challahconnection.com/faq.htm
NOTES: A brief article explaining how the Shabbat *challah* relates to manna, as well as blessings and recipes.

SITE: Question 7.7: What is the Significance of Challah
URL:
www.faqs.org/faqs/judaism/FAQ/04-Observance/section-36.html
NOTES: This article tells about the origin and importance of *challah*, and how it symbolizes the manna from the desert experience.

CATEGORY: Historical Ties
SUBJECT: Shtetl
EXPLANATION: Investigate how Shabbat was celebrated in the *shtetl*.

SITE: JewishGen ShtetLinks Directory
URL: www.shtetlinks.jewishgen.org
NOTES: This is the general site for locating information on *shtetls*. Links on the bottom of the page give you basic geographical regions, and from within any region you can choose from numerous *shtetls*. All are interesting, though some have more information and pictures than others.

SITE: ShtetLinks Page — Pilzno, Poland

URL: www.shtetlinks.jewishgen.org/pilzno/pilzno.html (see Figure 1-2, below)

NOTES: Lots of information about life in Pilzno, an excellent example of a *shtetl*. Be sure to read through the memoirs of its residents.

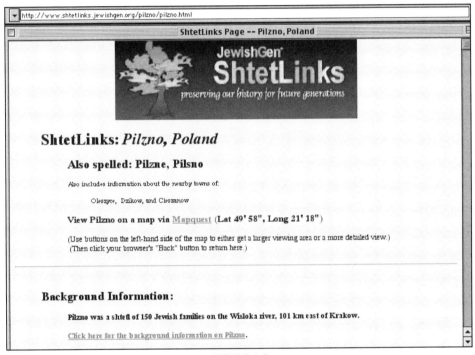

FIGURE 1-2

CATEGORY: Home Observance

SUBJECT: Ayshet Chayil — A Woman of Valor

EXPLANATION: As part of the Friday evening home ritual prior to dinner, the husband and children recite Proverbs 31:10-31 to their wife and mother. It is a sign of great honor and prestige to be called an *Ayshet Chayil.*

SITE: Aishes Chayil — Woman of Valor
URL: www.originaljudaica.com/ind/ac.html
NOTES: One artist's rendition of this *Ayshet Chayil*, with an explanation.

SITE: Family Time
URL: www.uscj.org/seabd/rockvilletic/education/familytime1.html
NOTES: An explanation of the home ceremony and the text of the prayer translated into English.

CATEGORY: Home Observance
SUBJECT: Birkat HaMazon
EXPLANATION: *Birkat Hamazon* is the Grace After Meals. Note that the special Shabbat version begins with *"Shir HaMa'alot."*

SITE: Birkat Hamazon
URL:
www.uahcweb.org/ny/tinw/ReligiousLiving/BirkatHamazon.htm
NOTES: The entire *Birkat Hamazon* is provided in Hebrew, English, and transliterated versions.

SITE: Grace After Meals
URL: www.bamidbar-shel.org/Birkat.htm
NOTES: An article explaining the practice and its origins.

CATEGORY: Home Observance
SUBJECT: Eliyahu HaNavi
EXPLANATION: *"Eliyahu HaNavi"* is a song that is sung at the end of Havdalah in the hope that the Messiah will soon arrive.

SITE: The Jewish Music Home Page
URL: www.jewishmusic.com
NOTES: Click on the link "Audio Library," then "Passover." You will be provided with numerous links to albums that contain the song. Explore, listen to clips using Real Audio, or purchase.

SITE: Zemerl — The Interactive Database of Jewish Song
URL: www.princeton.edu/zemerl
NOTES: Click on the link for "Pesakh" in the "Holiday" category, then scroll down and click on the song name in the left column. No sound clip is currently available.

CATEGORY: Home Observance
SUBJECT: Havdalah
EXPLANATION: *Havdalah* is the series of blessings recited at the end of Shabbat.

SITE: Havdalah — Ritual and Objects
URL: www.uahc.org/ny/tinw/ReligiousLiving/ReligiousObjects/
   HavdalahRO.htm (see Figure 1-3, below)
NOTES: An explanation and pictures of the ritual objects used in the Havdalah ceremony.

FIGURE 1-3

SITE: Works by Havdalah Set Artists
URL: www.artjudaica.com/cgi-bin/svend/gallery_havdalah
NOTES: Pictures of various types of Havdalah sets. Click on any thumbnail to view an enlarged photo.

CATEGORY: Personalities
SUBJECT: Ahad Ha'am
EXPLANATION: Ahad Ha'am was a famous Jewish thinker, writer, and Zionist leader who stated, "More than Jews have kept the Sabbath, the observance of the Sabbath has kept the Jews alive."

SITE: Ahad Ha-am
URL: www.encyclopedia.com/html/A/AhadH1aam.asp
NOTES: A short biography from encyclopedia.com.

SITE: Cultural Zionism
URL: store.yahoo.com/jewish146/polzion1.html
NOTES: A discussion of Ahad Ha'am's place within the development of Cultural Zionism.

CATEGORY: Prayers
SUBJECT: Amidah (Shemoneh Esray)
EXPLANATION: A special version of the *"Amidah"* is recited on Shabbat.

SITE: Hebrew Resources: The Amidah Prayer
URL: hebrewresources.com/amidah.html
NOTES: A lengthy overview of the *"Amidah,"* and a link where you can hear the prayer chanted.

SITE: The Transliterated Siddur
URL: siddur.org
NOTES: Scroll down and click on "Table of Contents," then on "The Weekday Morning Amidah."

CATEGORY: Prayers
SUBJECT: Kabbalat Shabbat
EXPLANATION: This series of prayers welcoming the Shabbat precede the *Ma'ariv* service on Friday night.

> **SITE:** Everything Jewish
> **URL:** www.everythingjewish.com
> **NOTES:** Click on "Laws & Customs" under "Jewish Holidays: Shabbat" in the menu at the left. You'll find a brief explanation of *Kabbalat Shabbat* and how it fits into the overall Shabbat experience.

> **SITE:** The Transliterated Siddur
> **URL:** siddur.com
> **NOTES:** Scroll down through the Table of Contents and select "Friday Night Service." Choose from the selections provided.

CATEGORY: Prayers
SUBJECT: L'cha Dodi
EXPLANATION: *"L'cha Dodi"* is a prayer welcoming the Sabbath bride. It is recited during the *Kabbalat Shabbat* service.

> **SITE:** The Jewish Music Home Page
> **URL:** www.jewishmusic.com
> **NOTES:** In the left column click on "Recordings," then on "Music Search." Then type "L'cha Dodi" in the "Song Name" box. You will be provided with numerous links to recordings that contain a version of this song; some of them may include a link to hear the song using Real Audio. Try alternate spellings (e.g., "Lecha Dodi") for more results.

> **SITE:** The Transliterated Siddur
> **URL:** siddur.com
> **NOTES:** Scroll down through the Table of Contents and select "Friday Night Service," then choose "L'cha Dodi."

CATEGORY: Ritual Objects
SUBJECT: Besamim — Spices
EXPLANATION: Spices are used in the Havdalah service as a reminder of the sweetness of Shabbat. The sweet fragrance reminds us of the "additional soul" that one has on Shabbat.

> **SITE:** Havdalah — Ritual and Objects
> **URL:** www.uahc.org/ny/tinw/ReligiousLiving/ReligiousObjects/
> HavdalahRO.htm
> **NOTES:** An explanation and pictures of the ritual objects used in the Havdalah ceremony.

> **SITE:** Works by Havdalah Set Artists
> **URL:** www.artjudaica.com/cgi-bin/svend/gallery_havdalah
> **NOTES:** Pictures of various types of Havdalah sets. Click on any thumbnail to view an enlarged photo.

CATEGORY: Ritual Objects
SUBJECT: Havdalah Set
EXPLANATION: A special braided candle, a spice box, and a Kiddush cup are used in the Havdalah ritual.

> **SITE:** Havdalah — Ritual and Objects
> **URL:** www.uahcweb.org/ny/tinw/ReligiousLiving/ReligiousObjects/
> HavdalahRO.htm
> **NOTES:** An explanation and pictures of the ritual objects used in the Havdalah ceremony, including the Havdalah blessings.

> **SITE:** Jewish Gifts from Judaica Worldwide
> **URL:** www.judaicaworldwide.com/judaica.asp
> **NOTES:** On this commercial site, scroll down and select "Havdalah sets" from the pull-down menu on the left. You'll find several pages of pictures of various types of sets. Click on any of them for an enlarged picture.

SITE: Jewish Bazaar — Havdalah Sets
URL: www.ipol.com/BAZAAR/Havdalah.HTM
NOTES: This commercial site includes numerous pictures of Havdalah sets. There is also a link to pictures of Havdalah candles.

CATEGORY: Ritual Objects
SUBJECT: Kiddush Cups
EXPLANATION: The *Kiddush* is a major part of every Shabbat dinner and the Friday evening service.

SITE: Candlesticks & Kiddish Cups
URL: www.nvo.com/menshenables/candlestickskiddishcups (see Figure 1-4, below)
NOTES: Scroll down through this commercial site for pictures of various traditional and modern *Kiddush* cups.

FIGURE 1-4

SITE: Kiddish Cups
URL: www.robinkimballdesigns.com/judaica/kiddish.htm
NOTES: This site contains a few pictures of modern *Kiddush* cups by the artist Robin Kimball.

SITE: Kiddush Cups Mile Chai Jewish Books and Judaica
URL: www.milechai.com/product/Kiddush_Cups.html
NOTES: This commercial site has photos of a number of traditional types of *Kiddush* cups. Click on the "Photos and Details" link under each picture for an enlarged example.

CATEGORY: Ritual Objects
SUBJECT: Shabbat Candles
EXPLANATION: Two candles are lit approximately 20 minutes prior to Shabbat.

SITE: Shabbat
URL: www.uahcweb.org/ny/tinw/ReligiousLiving/ReligiousObjects/
    Shabbat.htm
NOTES: This site provides numerous pictures and explanations as well as the blessing for the Shabbat candles.

SITE: Shabbat Candles: To See or Not to See
URL: www.ucalgary.ca/~elsegal/Shokel/951102_Two_Candles.html
NOTES: An article explaining the lighting of Shabbat candles.

CATEGORY: Texts
SUBJECT: Tanach Selections
EXPLANATION: Numerous passages from the Bible deal with or relate to Shabbat, including: Genesis 2:1-3, 48:20; Exodus 16:4-5, 13-26, 29, 20:8-11, 31:13-18; Numbers 6:24-26, 15:18-21; Deuteronomy 5:12; Isaiah 58:13-14; Psalm 92-93, 95-99, 104:14, 126; Proverbs 31:10-31; Ruth 4:12.

SITE: Divrei Torah – Commentaries
URL: shamash.org/tanach/dvar.shtml
NOTES: Scroll down for links to dozens of Torah commentary sites.

SITE: Navigating the Bible II
URL: bible.ort.org
NOTES: This site provides English and Hebrew versions of every Torah and Haftarah portion. Under "select language," click on English. On the next page, the "Translation" link will provide the full text in English that can be copied and pasted into a word processing program. The "Torah" and "Haftarot" links display limited sections of the Hebrew text as graphic images. These can be copied by right-clicking on the graphic, selecting "copy," then pasting the graphic into a word processing, page layout, or image editing document.

SITE: World Wide Study Bible
URL: www.ccel.org/wwsb
NOTES: Click on the link to the specific book that you want, then click on the correct chapter from the list of numbers. Scroll down to "More Scriptures" and click on "Jewish Bible." Choose from among the selections. The best English selection is the link "JPS." The "Hebrew" one requires a Hebrew reading font for your browser. All of these can be cut, pasted, and manipulated in a word processing program. Although the World Wide Study Bible is a Christian site, it has the only easily accessible online Bible text.

CATEGORY: Themes
SUBJECT: Tzedakah
EXPLANATION: It is traditional to give *tzedakah* just prior to Shabbat, and also to be thankful for God's gifts. Investigate *tzedakah* projects, both locally and in Israel, as well as ways to help the homeless.

SITE: 54 Ways You Can Help the Homeless
URL: www.earthsystems.org/ways (see Figure 1-5, below)
NOTES: This entire book is online and available for free download. It includes material on dozens of simple ways students and adults can help homeless people.

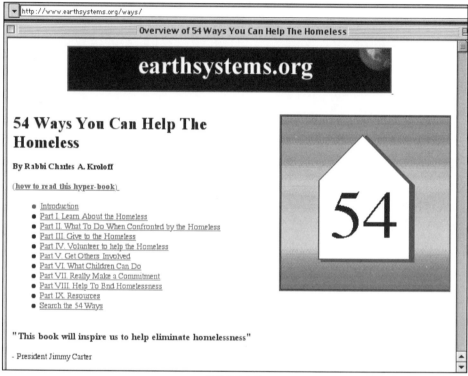

FIGURE 1-5

SITE: Volunteer Match
URL: www.volunteermatch.org
NOTES: Under "Find," enter your zip code and click "go." Then use the pull-down menus to specify how far you are willing to travel and what type of volunteer work you would like to do. Click "go" and choose from among the links presented, which include contact information.

SITE: Ziv Tzedakah Fund
URL: www.ziv.org
NOTES: Danny Siegel's *tzedakah* site includes a wealth of information and ideas for doing *mitzvot*. Scroll to the very bottom of the page and click on "116 Mitzvah Suggestions" for ideas.

CATEGORY: Themes
SUBJECT: Work Examples
EXPLANATION: Explore magazines and newspapers to find examples of activities that are allowed or prohibited on Shabbat.

SITE: Yahoo! News and Media: Magazines
URL: dir.yahoo.com/news_and_media/magazines
NOTES: Select first from the subject you desire, then select from numerous links to magazines around the country. Most of these have online versions of their text. Search through some of them to locate appropriate stories.

SITE: Yahoo! News and Media: Newspapers
URL: dir.yahoo.com/News_and_Media/Newspapers
NOTES: Scroll down to select from dozens of links to newspapers around the country. Most of these have online versions of their complete text. Search through some of them to locate appropriate stories.

Rosh Hashanah

CATEGORY: Arts
SUBJECT: Rosh Hashanah Music
EXPLANATION: Listen to music that was created for the themes and mood of the High Holy Days.

> **SITE:** The Jewish Music Home Page
> **URL:** www.jewishmusic.com
> **NOTES:** Click on the link "Audio Library," then "Holidays," then "High Holydays." Explore the numerous links to High Holy Day music, listen to clips using Real Audio, or purchase.

> **SITE:** Zemerl — The Interactive Database of Jewish Song
> **URL:** www.princeton.edu/zemerl
> **NOTES:** Click on the link for "High Holidays" in the "Holiday" category and select from the choices provided. Many have midi files for listening.

CATEGORY: Food
SUBJECT: Apples
EXPLANATION: Apples are eaten with honey to bring about a sweet year.

> **SITE:** Apples! Apples!
> **URL:** www.guilford.k12.nc.us/webquests/Apples/apples.htm (see Figure 1-6, opposite)
> **NOTES:** A teacher web site full of ideas, activities, and information about apples.

FIGURE 1-6

SITE: Apple Journal — "A Passion for Apples"
URL: www.applejournal.com
NOTES: This site contains almost everything you would want to know about apples. For photos of apples, click on the "Gallery" link under "Apple Archive" in the left side menu, then click on any of the "page" links in the first paragraph. Click on any thumbnail for an enlarged photo.

SITE: Washington State Apple Commission
URL: www.bestapples.com/new
NOTES: Select the "Apple Varieties" link, then click on one of the many thumbnail pictures for a larger view and information about a particular variety of apple.

CATEGORY: Food
SUBJECT: Challah
EXPLANATION: A special round *challah,* often with raisins, is eaten on Rosh HaShanah.

> **SITE:** Heritage — The Essence of Traditional Turbin (Round Challah)
> **URL:** www.tovaindustries.com/Challah/turban.htm
> **NOTES:** Instructions and diagrams showing how to make a round holiday *challah.*

> **SITE:** Rosh HaShana Recipe — Round Raisin Challah
> **URL:** judaism.about.com/library/food/blrhroundchallah.htm
> **NOTES:** A detailed recipe for making a round holiday *challah.*

CATEGORY: Food
SUBJECT: Honey
EXPLANATION: Honey is eaten with apples to bring about a sweet year.

> **SITE:** Honey.com — The Honey Expert
> **URL:** www.honey.com
> **NOTES:** Everything you might want to know about honey, including pictures, information, "kids' stuff," recipes, and more.

> **SITE:** Welcome To Burleson's Honey
> **URL:** www.burlesons-honey.com
> **NOTES:** Another site with a wealth of information about honey: pictures, information, "kids' stuff," recipes, and more.

CATEGORY: Food
SUBJECT: Rosh Hashanah Dishes
EXPLANATION: Use these sites to locate a number of High Holy Day recipes.

SITE: Jewish Food Mailing List Archives
URL: jewishfood-list.com
NOTES: Click on the "Recipes" link and select from among the choices provided.

SITE: Mimi's Cyber-Kitchen
URL: www.cyber-kitchen.com (see Figure 1-7, below)
NOTES: Click on "Mimi's Recipes," then scroll down to the "Holiday Central" link on the left-hand side. Click on "Jewish High Holidays" and choose from over a dozen links to holiday recipes.

FIGURE 1-7

CATEGORY: Home Observance
SUBJECT: Electronic Greeting Cards
EXPLANATION: Create and send electronic New Year's cards to family members and friends.

SITE: Blue Mountain — The World's Favorite eCards
URL: www.bluemountain.com
NOTES: To send anyone online a greeting, choose from the categories in the left column from dozens of choices. There is a limited selection of free cards, and a much larger selection of cards for purchase. With dozens of choices, this is probably the largest collection of e-cards on the Internet.

SITE: Yahoo! Greetings
URL: greetings.yahoo.com
NOTES: Send anyone a free online greeting. Choose from a variety of themes such as Holidays, Birthdays, Love, Events, and Wishes and Thoughts.

CATEGORY: Miscellaneous
SUBJECT: Magazines/Newspapers
EXPLANATION: Search for pictures and articles that deal with Rosh HaShanah and the High Holy Days in general.

SITE: Yahoo! News and Media: Magazines
URL: dir.yahoo.com/news_and_media/magazines
NOTES: Select first from the subject you desire, then select from numerous links to magazines around the country. Most have online versions of their text. Search through some of them to locate the appropriate information.

SITE: Yahoo! News and Media: Newspapers
URL: dir.yahoo.com/News_and_Media/Newspapers
NOTES: Scroll down to select from dozens of links to newspapers around the country. Most have online versions of their complete text. Search through some of them to locate the appropriate information.

CATEGORY: Personalities
SUBJECT: Saadia Gaon
EXPLANATION: Saadia Gaon was a tenth century scholar who developed ten reasons for sounding the *shofar* during the Days of Awe.

SITE: Saadia Gaon
URL: scheinerman.net/judaism/teens/personalities/saadia1.html
NOTES: Lots of information on Saadia Gaon from the Jewish Teen Page.

CATEGORY: Prayers
SUBJECT: Avinu Malkaynu
EXPLANATION: *"Avinu Malkaynu"* is one of the best known prayers in the High Holy Day liturgy.

SITE: Yom Kippur — Jewish Day of Atonement
URL: judaism.about.com/library/holidays/higholidays/bl_yk.htm
NOTES: Select the link for "Prayers" from the top menu. Read about the prayer *"Avinu Malkaynu"* as part of the Yom Kippur liturgy.

CATEGORY: Prayers
SUBJECT: Hineni
EXPLANATION: *"Hineni"* is a dramatic prayer recited by the Rabbi or Cantor as part of the *erev* Rosh HaShanah service.

SITE: Urim v'Tumim Online
URL: www.yale.edu/uvt/fall97/hirsch.html
NOTES: Background on the *"Hineni"* prayer, including biblical sources.

CATEGORY: Prayers
SUBJECT: Un'Taneh Tokef
EXPLANATION: *"Un'Taneh Tokef"* is an important prayer describing the heavenly day of judgment.

SITE: JewishGates.org
URL: jewishgates.efficientweb.com/file.asp?File_ID=518
NOTES: Scroll down to the sixth paragraph to read about the significance of this prayer.

CATEGORY: Ritual Objects
SUBJECT: Shofar
EXPLANATION: The *shofar* is a ram's horn blown on the High Holy Days.

SITE: Judaica Online Shofars
URL: www.judaicaonline.com/CT_Misc/PRMS2_MSG427.htm
NOTES: A number of pictures of *shofarot* are provided on this commercial site.

SITE: Shofar
URL: www.uahcweb.org/ny/tinw/ReligiousLiving/ReligiousObjects/
Shofar.htm (see Figure 1-8, below)
NOTES: This site contains numerous pictures and explanations, as well as the blessings for the blowing of the *shofar*. Also included are links to wav files to listen to the *shofar* calls.

FIGURE 1-8

CATEGORY: Texts
SUBJECT: Tanach Selections
EXPLANATION: Numerous biblical passages relate to Rosh HaShanah. These include selections that mention or explore the themes of the holiday, as well as the Torah/Haftarah portions associated with the holiday (traditional and Reform). Be sure to explore: Genesis 1:21-22; Exodus 19:16-19, 20:15-18; Leviticus 23:23-24; Numbers 29:1-6; I Samuel 1:1-2:10; Amos 3:6, Ezekiel 33:4-5, Isaiah 27:13, 58:6-13; Jeremiah 31:2-20; Micah 7:19; Zechariah 9:14-16; Zephaniah 1:14-16; Ezra 3:6; Nehemiah 8:1-11, Psalms 81:4-5, 88:6, 150.

SITE: Divrei Torah — Commentaries
URL: shamash.org/tanach/dvar.shtml
NOTES: Scroll down for links to dozens of Torah commentary sites.

SITE: Navigating the Bible II
URL: bible.ort.org
NOTES: This site provides English and Hebrew versions of every Torah and Haftarah portion. Under "select language," click on English. On the next page, the "Translation" link will provide the full text in English that can be copied and pasted into a word processing program. The "Torah" and "Haftarot" links display limited sections of the Hebrew text as graphic images. These can be copied by right-clicking on the graphic, selecting "copy," then pasting the graphic into a word processing, page layout, or image editing document.

SITE: World Wide Study Bible
URL: www.ccel.org/wwsb
NOTES: Click on the link to the specific book that you want, then click on the correct chapter from the list of numbers. Scroll down to "More Scriptures" and click on "Jewish Bible." Choose from among the selections. The best English selection is the link "JPS." The "Hebrew" one requires a Hebrew-reading font for your browser. All of these can be cut, pasted and manipulated in a word processing program. Although the World Wide Study Bible is a Christian site, it has the only easily accessible online Bible text.

CATEGORY: Themes
SUBJECT: Children's Literature
EXPLANATION: Locate stories about children not behaving nicely. Temporarily omit the ending and discuss what the child in the story might have done differently.

> **SITE:** Children's Literature Web Site
> **URL:** www.ucalgary.ca/~dkbrown/index.html
> **NOTES:** Search under the "More Links" section for descriptions of various pieces of literature.

> **SITE:** Database of Award-Winning Children's Literature
> **URL:** www.dawcl.com
> **NOTES:** Click on the link for "Search Database" and select the type of literature in which you are interested.

CATEGORY: Themes
SUBJECT: Kittel
EXPLANATION: The *kittel* is a white garment worn on the High Holy Days.

> **SITE:** Ahavat Israel — Yom Kippur
> **URL:** www.ahavat-israel.com/ahavat/torat/yomkippur.asp
> **NOTES:** Scroll down to the "White Garment" section for a description of the use of the *kittel*.

CATEGORY: Themes
SUBJECT: World
EXPLANATION: Rosh HaShanah commemorates the creation of the world. One of the themes is the idea that we are partners with God in the creation of the world, and that creation is not yet finished. Locate pictures of the beauty and diversity of creation.

SITE: Ditto.com
URL: ditto.com
NOTES: Type "earth from space" in the search box and click "GO." You will be provided with a number of thumbnails of pictures taken by astronauts. Click on any thumbnail for an enlarged photo.

SITE: The History Place — Best of Ansel Adams
URL: www.historyplace.com/unitedstates/adams/index.html (see Figure 1-9, below)
NOTES: Select from 25 of the photographer's favorite photos of scenic America.

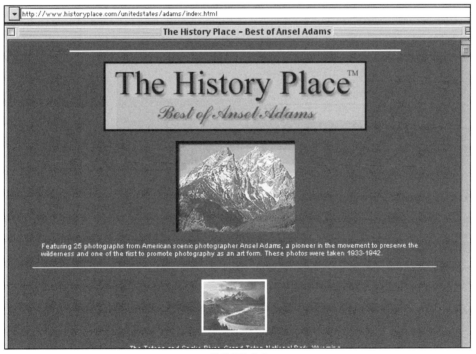

FIGURE 1-9

SITE: Yosemite Photo Album and 3D Trail Guide
URL: www.n2.net/freemapsin3d/yosemite
NOTES: Download pictures and scroll down to select links to photos of some of the most beautiful examples of nature in the U.S.

Yom Kippur

CATEGORY: Arts
SUBJECT: Yom Kippur Music
EXPLANATION: Listen to music that was created for the themes and mood of the High Holy Days.

> **SITE:** The Jewish Music Home Page
> **URL:** www.jewishmusic.com
> **NOTES:** Click on the link "Audio Library," then "Holidays," then "High Holydays." Explore the numerous links to Yom Kippur music, listen to clips using Real Audio, or purchase.

> **SITE:** Zemerl — The Interactive Database of Jewish Song
> **URL:** www.princeton.edu/zemerl (see Figure 1-10, opposite)
> **NOTES:** Click on the link for "High Holidays" in the "Holiday" category, and select from the choices provided. Many have midi files for listening.

CATEGORY: Food
SUBJECT: Challah
EXPLANATION: A special round *challah* (often with raisins) is eaten prior to and after the Yom Kippur fast.

> **SITE:** Heritage — The Essence of Traditional Turbin (Round Challah)
> **URL:** www.tovaindustries.com/Challah/turban.htm
> **NOTES:** Instructions and diagrams showing how to make a round holiday *challah*.

> **SITE:** Rosh HaShana Recipe — Round Raisin Challah
> **URL:** judaism.about.com/library/food/blrhroundchallah.htm
> **NOTES:** A detailed recipe for making a round holiday *challah*.

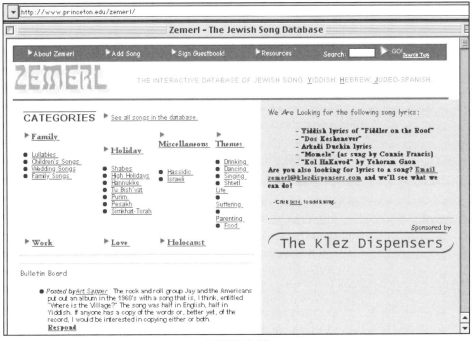

FIGURE 1-10

CATEGORY: Personalities

SUBJECT: Hillel

EXPLANATION: Hillel tried to maintain a balance between self and the rest of the world: "If I am not for myself, who will be for me? If I am for myself alone, what am I? If not now, when?" This theme is something to consider during Yom Kippur.

> **SITE:** Jewish Virtual Library: Hillel and Shammai
>
> **URL:** www.us-israel.org/jsource/biography/hillel.html
>
> **NOTES:** Information on Hillel's life from the American-Israeli Cooperative Enterprise.

> **SITE:** Sages and Scholars
>
> **URL:** www.nottm.edu.org.uk/jewfaq/sages.htm#Hillel
>
> **NOTES:** A brief introduction to Hillel and Shammai.

CATEGORY: Prayers
SUBJECT: Al Chayt
EXPLANATION: *"Al Chayt"* is one of the prayers in the confessional.

SITE: Judaism 101: Yom Kippur
URL: www.jewfaq.org/holiday4.htm
NOTES: Scroll down to the "Yom Kippur Liturgy" section to read about the Al Chayt prayer.

SITE: Yom Kippur — Jewish Day of Atonement
URL: judaism.about.com/library/holidays/higholidays/bl_yk.htm
NOTES: Select the "Prayers" link from the top menu. Scroll down several paragraphs to read about the *"Al Chayt"* prayer as part of the Yom Kippur liturgy.

CATEGORY: Prayers
SUBJECT: Ashamnu
EXPLANATION: *"Ashamnu"* is one of the prayers in the confessional.

SITE: Benedictions, Blessings, Laws, Liturgical Hymns/Poems, Prayers, Psalms
URL: www.rrz.uni-hamburg.de/rz3a035/service.html
NOTES: A short explanation of the *"Ashamnu"* prayer.

SITE: Judaism 101: Yom Kippur
URL: www.jewfaq.org/holiday4.htm
NOTES: Scroll down to the "Yom Kippur Liturgy" section to read about the *"Ashamnu"* prayer.

SITE: Yom Kippur — Jewish Day of Atonement
URL: judaism.about.com/library/holidays/higholidays/bl_yk.htm
NOTES: Select the "Prayers" link from the top menu. Read about the *"Ashamnu"* prayer as part of the Yom Kippur liturgy.

CATEGORY: Prayers
SUBJECT: Ki Anu Amecha
EXPLANATION: *"Ki Anu Amecha"* is a prayer that asks God to forgive our failings.

> **SITE:** Mouth to Mouth with God
> **URL:** www.shalomctr.org/html/seas37.html
> **NOTES:** A short explanation of the theme of the prayer.

> **SITE:** Yom Kippur Survival Kit — Torah.org
> **URL:** www.torah.org/learning/yomtov/yomkippur/yksurvival5.html
> **NOTES:** Scroll down for a short explanation of the significance of the prayer within the liturgy.

CATEGORY: Prayers
SUBJECT: Kol Nidre
EXPLANATION: The best known of all Yom Kippur prayers, *"Kol Nidre"* is sung or recited three times at the beginning of the Ma'ariv service.

> **SITE:** Yom Kippur — Jewish Day of Atonement
> **URL:** judaism.about.com/library/holidays/higholidays/bl_yk.htm
> **NOTES:** Select the "Prayers" link from the top menu. Read about the *"Kol Nidre"* prayer as part of the Yom Kippur liturgy.

> **SITE:** Yom Kippur—Torah.org
> **URL:** torah.org/learning/yomtov/yomkippur (see Figure 1-11, p. 32)
> **NOTES:** Click on the link for *"Kol Nidre"* for an explanation of the theme of the prayer.

CATEGORY: Prayers
SUBJECT: Sh'ma Kolaynu
EXPLANATION: "Hear our voice," *"Sh'ma Kolaynu"* is a prayer recited near the end of the Yom Kippur service.

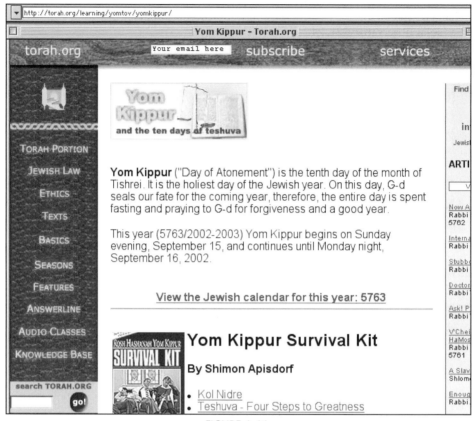

FIGURE 1-11

SITE: The Jewish Music Home Page

URL: www.jewishmusic.com

NOTES: Click on the link "Audio Library," then "Holidays," then "High Holydays." Explore the numerous links to Yom Kippur music, listen to clips using Real Audio, or purchase.

SITE: Selichos

URL: www.flash.net/~tiermacw/selichos.htm

NOTES: A lengthy scholarly article about *Selichot* that discusses the *"Sh'ma Kolaynu"* prayer in easy to read terms. Scroll down to the third paragraph.

CATEGORY: Prayers
SUBJECT: Yizkor
EXPLANATION: *Yizkor* is the memorial service held on Yom Kippur and on the last day of each of the three Festivals.

> **SITE:** Guide to the Jewish Funeral
> **URL:** www.jewish-funerals.org/brochure.htm
> **NOTES:** Information about all aspects of the Jewish funeral and Jewish burial practices.

> **SITE:** Yizkor — Remembrance of the Departed
> **URL:** www.yahrzeit.org/yizkor.html
> **NOTES:** An entire site devoted to *Yizkor*. Choose from the many links on the side or bottom for a wealth of information on *Yizkor* practices.

CATEGORY: Ritual Objects
SUBJECT: Shofar
EXPLANATION: The *shofar* is a ram's horn blown to signal the end of Yom Kippur.

> **SITE:** Judaica Online Shofars
> **URL:** www.judaicaonline.com/CT_Misc/PRMS2_MSG427.htm
> **NOTES:** A number of pictures of *shofarot* are provided on this commercial site.

> **SITE:** Shofar
> **URL:** www.uahcweb.org/ny/tinw/ReligiousLiving/ReligiousObjects/
>   Shofar.htm
> **NOTES:** This site contains numerous pictures and explanations, as well as the blessings for the blowing of the *shofar*. Also included are links to wav files to listen to the *shofar* call.

CATEGORY: Texts
SUBJECT: Tanach Selections
EXPLANATION: Many biblical passages deal with or relate to Yom Kippur. These include selections that mention or explain the themes of the holiday, as well as the Torah/Haftarah portions associated with the holiday (traditional and Reform). Be sure to explore: Leviticus 16, 18:1-30, 19:1-37, 23:27-32, 25:9-10; Numbers 29:7-11; Deuteronomy 29:9-14, 30:11-20; Isaiah 1:18, 57:14-58:14; Jonah; Micah 7:18-20.

SITE: Divrei Torah – Commentaries
URL: shamash.org/tanach/dvar.shtml
NOTES: Scroll down for links to dozens of Torah commentary sites.

SITE: Navigating the Bible II
URL: bible.ort.org
NOTES: This site provides English and Hebrew versions of every Torah and Haftarah portion. Under "select language," click on English. On the next page, the "Translation" link will provide the full text in English that can be copied and pasted into a word processing program. The "Torah" and "Haftarot" links display limited sections of the Hebrew text as graphic images. These can be copied by right-clicking on the graphic, selecting "copy," then pasting the graphic into a word processing, page layout, or image editing document.

SITE: World Wide Study Bible
URL: www.ccel.org/wwsb
NOTES: Click on the link to the specific book that you want, then click on the correct chapter from the list of numbers. Scroll down to "More Scriptures" and click on "Jewish Bible." Choose from among the selections. The best English selection is the link "JPS." The "Hebrew" one requires a Hebrew-reading font for your browser. All of these can be cut, pasted, and manipulated in a word processing program. Although the World Wide Study Bible is a Christian site, it has the only easily accessible online Bible text.

CATEGORY: Themes
SUBJECT: Kittel
EXPLANATION: A *kittel* is a white garment worn on the High Holy Days.

> **SITE:** Ahavat Israel — Yom Kippur
> **URL:** www.ahavat-israel.com/ahavat/torat/yomkippur.asp
> **NOTES:** Scroll down to the "White Garment" section for a description of the use of the *kittel.*

CATEGORY: Themes
SUBJECT: Scapegoat — Azazel
EXPLANATION: The concept of the scapegoat originated with Aaron, the High Priest, "placing the sins" of Israel upon a goat and sending it (letting it "escape") into the wilderness.

> **SITE:** Mountain Goat
> **URL:** www.bcadventures.com/adventure/wilderness/animals/
> mntgoat.htm (see Figure 1-12, p. 36)
> **NOTES:** Some basic information about mountain goats, including a photo.

> **SITE:** Scapegoating Research & Remedies
> **URL:** www.scapegoat.demon.co.uk
> **NOTES:** A lengthy discussion on the concepts of scapegoats as they affect human society.

> **SITE:** Sin Offering
> **URL:** webstu.messiah.edu/~kc1176/sin_offering.html
> **NOTES:** A picture of the goat and explanation of the sin offering with Tanach references. Although the URL suggests that this is a Christian or Messianic site, there is no mention of this affiliation on this page or on the main page of the site.

FIGURE 1-12

CATEGORY: Themes
SUBJECT: Tzedakah
EXPLANATION: It is traditional to give *tzedakah* on Yom Kippur. Investigate *tzedakah* projects, both locally and in Israel, as well as ways to help the homeless.

> **SITE:** 54 Ways You Can Help the Homeless
> **URL:** www.earthsystems.org/ways
> **NOTES:** This entire book is online and available for free download. It includes material on dozens of simple ways students and adults can help homeless people.

SITE: Volunteer Match

URL: www.volunteermatch.org (see Figure 1-13, below)

NOTES: Under "Find," enter your zip code and click "go." Then use the pull-down menus to specify how far you are willing to travel and what type of volunteer work you would like to do. Click "go" and choose from among the links presented, which include contact information.

FIGURE 1-13

SITE: Ziv Tzedakah Fund

URL: www.ziv.org

NOTES: Danny Siegel's *tzedakah* site includes a wealth of information and ideas for doing *mitzvot*. Scroll to the very bottom of the page and click on "116 Mitzvah Suggestions" for ideas.

Sukkot and Hoshana Rabbah

CATEGORY: Historical Ties
SUBJECT: The Harvest Season
EXPLANATION: Investigate why Sukkot falls during the harvest season.

> **SITE:** SUCCOT: To KNOW, or to REMEMBER
> **URL:** www.tanach.org/special/succot.txt
> **NOTES:** An interesting discussion of the observance of Sukkot, and why we celebrate it at the time of the harvest.

CATEGORY: Maps
SUBJECT: Israel — Ancient
EXPLANATION: Locate Jerusalem and other cities on a map of Israel. The Israelites traveled to Jerusalem to sacrifice at the Temple during Sukkot, one of the pilgrimage festivals.

> **SITE:** Bible Maps of Bible Times and Lands
> **URL:** www.bible.ca/maps
> **NOTES:** Choose from among several maps of ancient Israel. Note that this is a Christian site.

> **SITE:** The Hebrews: The Major Cities and Regions
> **URL:** www.wsu.edu/~dee/HEBREWS/ANISRMAP.HTM
> **NOTES:** A map of the major biblical cities and regions of ancient Israel.

CATEGORY: Miscellaneous
SUBJECT: Phases of the Moon
EXPLANATION: The Hebrew calendar is based on the phases of the moon. Sukkot begins on the full moon.

SITE: Earth and Moon Viewer
URL: www.fourmilab.ch/earthview/vplanet.html
NOTES: Lots of pictures, information, and links to material about the moon.

SITE: The Moon
URL: www.netaxs.com/~mhmyers/moon.tn.html
NOTES: Numerous photographs of the various phases of the moon.

SITE: Virtual Reality Moon Phases Pictures
URL: tycho.usno.navy.mil/vphase.html
NOTES: View images of the phases of the moon for any date in modern history.

CATEGORY: Prayers
SUBJECT: Hallel
EXPLANATION: The Hallel, recited during Festivals, consists of Psalms 113-118.

SITE: Hallel — "Praise of G-D" — OU.ORG
URL: www.ou.org/chagim/hallel.htm
NOTES: The site includes a detailed explanation of the development of the Hallel section and how and when it is recited.

CATEGORY: Prayers
SUBJECT: Yizkor
EXPLANATION: *Yizkor* is the memorial service held on Yom Kippur and on the last day of each of the three Festivals.

SITE: Guide to the Jewish Funeral
URL: www.jewish-funerals.org/brochure.htm
NOTES: Information about all aspects of the Jewish funeral and Jewish burial practices.

SITE: Yizkor — Remembrance of the Departed
URL: www.yahrzeit.org/yizkor.html
NOTES: An entire site devoted to *Yizkor*. Choose from the many links on the side or bottom for a wealth of information on *Yizkor* practices.

CATEGORY: Ritual Objects
SUBJECT: Aravah — Willow
EXPLANATION: The *aravah*, the willow, is one of the four species. It has neither taste nor aroma.

SITE: Hoshana Rabbah
URL: www.tckillian.com:8080/greg/hoshana.html
NOTES: A lengthy explanation of the customs, laws, and *midrashim* related to the *aravah*, as well as its uses.

SITE: Hoshana Rabbah at OU.ORG
URL: www.ou.org/chagim/sukkot/hoshana.htm
NOTES: An explanation of how the *aravah* is used on *Hoshana Rabbah*.

SITE: Weeping Willow
URL: cas.bellarmine.edu/robinson/weeping.htm
NOTES: A picture and description of the willow tree, with links to other examples.

CATEGORY: Ritual Objects
SUBJECT: Etrog
EXPLANATION: The *etrog* is one of the four species. It has both taste and aroma.

SITE: Israeli Etrogim Center
URL: www.israeletrogcenter.com (see Figure 1-14, opposite)
NOTES: Pictures and basic information on the *etrog*. The site is full of pop-up ads that you will need to close.

FIGURE 1-14

SITE: Sukkot on the Net — Etrog, Lulav and The Four Species
URL: www.holidays.net/sukkot/symbols.htm
NOTES: Basic information and pictures of the other four species, including the *etrog*.

SITE: Zaide Reuven's Esrog Farm
URL: members.aol.com/zrsesrog
NOTES: Information and pictures of *etrog* trees from the web site of an *etrog* farm.

CATEGORY: Ritual Objects
SUBJECT: Hadas — Myrtle
EXPLANATION: *Hadas*, the myrtle, is one of the four species. It has aroma but no taste.

SITE: Crape Myrtle Farm
URL: www.crapemyrtles.net
NOTES: Scroll down to the numerous thumbnail pictures of a variety of myrtle trees. Click on any of the pictures for a full view.

SITE: Sukkot on the Net — Etrog, Lulav and The Four Species
URL: www.holidays.net/sukkot/symbols.htm
NOTES: Basic information and pictures of the four species, including the *hadas*.

CATEGORY: Ritual Objects
SUBJECT: Lulav
EXPLANATION: The *lulav* is the name given to the three-part branched object comprised of the myrtle *(hadas)*, the willow *(aravah)*, and the palm *(lulav)*.

SITE: Lulav and Etrog
URL: uahc.org/ny/tinw/ReligiousLiving/ReligiousObjects/
    LulavEtrog.htm (see Figure 1-15, opposite)
NOTES: This site includes pictures and explanations, as well as the blessings over the *lulav*.

SITE: The Lulav and Etrog — Sukkot at OU.ORG
URL: www.ou.org/chagim/sukkot/lulavetrog.htm
NOTES: Pictures and explanations of the *lulav* and *etrog*.

SITE: Sukkot on the Net — Etrog, Lulav, and The Four Species
URL: www.holidays.net/sukkot/symbols.htm
NOTES: Basic information and pictures of the *lulav* and the other three of the four species.

CATEGORY: Ritual Objects
SUBJECT: Lulav — Palm
EXPLANATION: The *lulav* — the palm — is one of the four species. It has taste but no aroma.

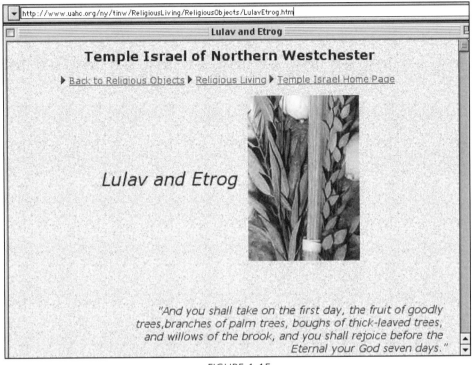

FIGURE 1-15

SITE: Palm Trees Gallery
URL: www.gardencomposer.com.au/dicomp-gallery-2.html (see Figure 1-16, p. 44)
NOTES: The site provides numerous pictures of various types of palm trees. Click on the thumbnail pictures to enlarge them to full size.

SITE: Sukkot on the Net — Etrog, Lulav, and The Four Species
URL: www.holidays.net/sukkot/symbols.htm
NOTES: Basic information and pictures of the four species, including the *lulav.*

FIGURE 1-16

CATEGORY: Texts
SUBJECT: Tanach Selections
EXPLANATION: Many biblical passages relate to Sukkot. These include selections that mention the holiday or explain its themes, as well as the Torah/Haftarah portions associated with the holiday (traditional and Reform). Be sure to explore: Exodus 23:14-17, 33-44, 33:12-34:26; Leviticus 22:26-23:44; Numbers 28:12-16, 29:12-16, 20-35-30:1; Deuteronomy 11:10-15, 14:22-16:17, 20:19, 31:10-13; I Kings 8:2-21; Ezekiel 38:18-39:16; Zechariah 14:1-21; Ecclesiastes; Nehemiah 8:14-18; Psalms 24:1, 47, 93, 96-99, 118:25.

SITE: Divrei Torah — Commentaries
URL: shamash.org/tanach/dvar.shtml
NOTES: Scroll down for links to dozens of Torah commentary sites.

SITE: Navigating the Bible II
URL: bible.ort.org
NOTES: This site provides English and Hebrew versions of every Torah and Haftarah portion. Under "select language," click on English. On the next page, the "Translation" link will provide the full text in English that can be copied and pasted into a word processing program. The "Torah" and "Haftarot" links display limited sections of the Hebrew text as graphic images. These can be copied by right-clicking on the graphic, selecting "copy," then pasting the graphic into a word processing, page layout, or image editing document.

SITE: World Wide Study Bible
URL: www.ccel.org/wwsb
NOTES: Click on the link to the specific book that you want, then click on the correct chapter from the list of numbers. Scroll down to "More Scriptures" and click on "Jewish Bible." Choose from among the selections. The best English selection is the link "JPS." The "Hebrew" one requires a Hebrew-reading font for your browser. All of these can be cut, pasted, and manipulated in a word processing program. Although the World Wide Study Bible is a Christian site, it has the only easily accessible online Bible text.

CATEGORY: Themes
SUBJECT: Farms
EXPLANATION: The results of the harvest can be seen on American farms.

SITE: Farm Animals
URL: www.kidsfarm.com/farm.htm
NOTES: Pictures and information about farm animals.

SITE: Farmphoto.com
URL: www.farmphoto.com/homestead/forum.asp
NOTES: Hundreds of photos of farms. Select from the subject menu on the left, and click on any thumbnail to view an enlarged photo.

SITE: Living History Farms; Get Your Grip on History
URL: www.lhf.org (see Figure 1-17, below)
NOTES: Click on the links in the "Take a Tour" section near the bottom of the page to explore farms throughout American history.

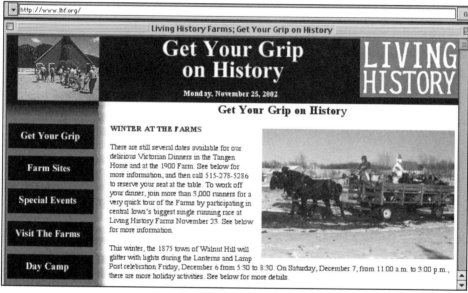

FIGURE 1-17

CATEGORY: Themes
SUBJECT: Tents
EXPLANATION: The sukkah is based on the dwellings that the Israelites built in the desert. They may have been similar to contemporary Bedouin tents.

SITE: Photographic Exhibit — The Bedouin
URL: medic.bgu.ac.il/bedouin
NOTES: Click on the link to "Nomadic Tribes" for a set of photos.

SITE: Sinai — The Bedouin Way
URL: www.interknowledge.com/egypt/sinai/bedouin02.htm (see Figure 1-18, below)
NOTES: Information about and pictures of Bedouin tents.

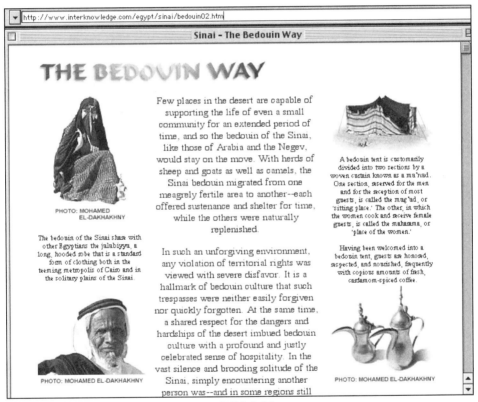

FIGURE 1-18

Shemini Atzeret and Simchat Torah

CATEGORY: Arts
SUBJECT: Marc Chagall
EXPLANATION: Marc Chagall was a famous Jewish artist. Some of his works featured people rejoicing with the Torah.

> **SITE:** Chagall Windows on Exhibition
> **URL:** www.hadassah.org.il/chagall.htm
> **NOTES:** This is the official web site for the Chagall Windows at the Hadassah-Hebrew University Medical Center in Israel. The site includes information about the windows, their development, biographical material about Chagall, and links to additional Chagall sites.

> **SITE:** The Knesset — The Parliament of Israel
> **URL:** www.knesset.gov.il/main/eng/engframe.htm
> **NOTES:** Click on "Knesset Tour" in the top row of icons, then on "Chagall State Hall" for an explanation of the Chagall tapestries and mosaics that decorate this reception area. One of these tapestries features the image of King David carrying the Torah — click on the first photo for a better view.

CATEGORY: Arts
SUBJECT: Yehudit Yellin
EXPLANATION: Yehudit Yellin is an Israeli painter. Some of her works featured people rejoicing with the Torah.

SITE: Judith Yellin-Ginat, Israeli Painter and Artist

URL: www.israelartguide.co.il/yellin/index.htm (see Figure 1-19, below)

NOTES: This site contains some examples of Yellin-Ginat's work. Click on "Exhibition:," then on "Simchat Torah" in the left column. Click on any of the thumbnails to view an enlarged picture.

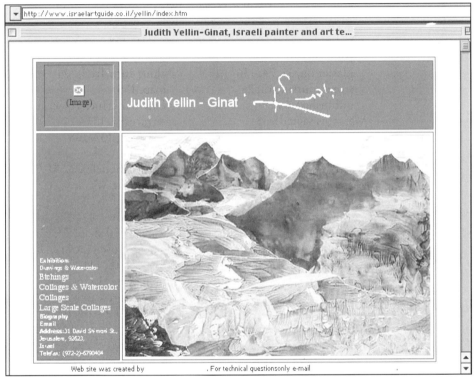

FIGURE 1-19

CATEGORY: Maps

SUBJECT: Babylonia and Palestine

EXPLANATION: Explore the location of Babylonia in relation to Palestine. There was a struggle for leadership in the Jewish world between these two communities after the *Mishnah* was completed.

SITE: Bible Maps of Bible Times and Lands
URL: www.bible.ca/maps
NOTES: Choose from among several maps of ancient Israel, Babylonia, and Palestine. Note that this is a Christian site.

SITE: World.jpg
URL: www.khouse.org/blueletter/images/maps/Otest/world.jpg (see Figure 1-20, below)
NOTES: An ancient map of Babylonia, Palestine, and the Middle East.

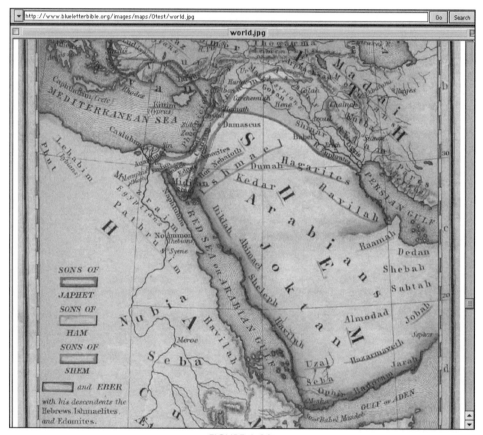

FIGURE 1-20

CATEGORY: Miscellaneous
SUBJECT: Israeli Flag
EXPLANATION: Israeli flags are customarily waved by children during the Simchat Torah celebration.

SITE: The Flag and the Emblem
URL: www.israel-mfa.gov.il/mfa/go.asp?MFAH0cph0
NOTES: This site, which is sponsored by Israel's Ministry of Foreign Affairs, features an essay on the history of the Israeli flag.

SITE: Israeli Flags Geographic.org
URL: www.geographic.org/flags/israel_flags.html
NOTES: A simple picture of an Israeli flag. Also included is a photo of an Israeli athlete carrying the flag at the 2000 Olympics.

SITE: The New Israel Shop
URL: www.israelshop1.com
NOTES: Click on the link for "Israeli flags" and select from a variety of sizes, shapes, and designs.

CATEGORY: Miscellaneous
SUBJECT: Pomegranate
EXPLANATION: The *rimmonim* of the Torah are often shaped like pomegranates.

SITE: Chadmark Farms Pomegranates
URL: www.tcsn.net/chadmark/pomegranate.htm
NOTES: Pictures of and information about pomegranates.

SITE: Gernot Katzer's Spice Dictionary
URL: www-ang.kfunigraz.ac.at/~katzer/engl/
generic_frame.html?Puni_gra.html
NOTES: A site devoted to information about and pictures of pomegranates.

CATEGORY: Miscellaneous
SUBJECT: Twelve Tribes
EXPLANATION: Symbols of the 12 tribes are often used to decorate Simchat Torah flags. Find artwork depicting these symbols.

SITE: Chagall Windows
URL: www.hadassah.org.il/chagall.htm (see Figure 1-21, below)
NOTES: This is the official web site for the Chagall Windows at the Hadassah-Hebrew University Medical Center in Israel. The site includes information about the windows, their development, and the symbolism found in each tribe's window.

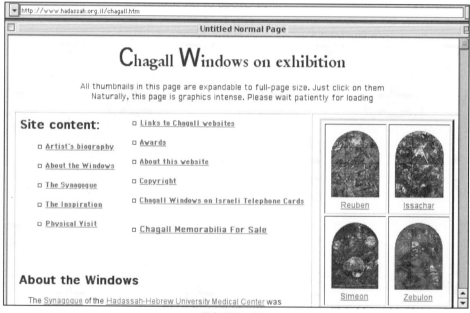

FIGURE 1-21

SITE: The Twelve Tribes of Israel
URL: www.wzo.org.il/juice/map/map1.htm
NOTES: A simple map of the approximate locations of the Twelve Tribes.

SITE: Windows — the Twelve Tribes
URL: www.templebethelaptos.org/windows/index.html
NOTES: Photos and descriptions from a synagogue in California of contemporary stained glass windows depicting the tribes. Click on the name of any tribe for detailed information about the tribe and its symbols.

CATEGORY: Places
SUBJECT: Kotel
EXPLANATION: The *Kotel* in Jerusalem is the center of action during Simchat Torah celebrations.

SITE: Live Western Wall Camera at Aish HaTorah
URL: www.aish.com/wallcam
NOTES: Get a real time picture of the *Kotel*. Click "Enlarge View" for a full-screen picture.

SITE: Virtual Israel Experience
URL: www.us-israel.org/jsource/vie/Jerutoc.html
NOTES: Pictures, information, and links to every part of Jerusalem. Select from the many links provided, both within the text and at the bottom of the page.

CATEGORY: Prayers
SUBJECT: Amidah
EXPLANATION: The blessing for rain is added to the *"Amidah"* beginning on Shemini Atzeret.

SITE: Hebrew Resources: The Amidah Prayer
URL: hebrewresources.com/amidah.html
NOTES: A lengthy overview of the *"Amidah,"* and a link where you can hear the prayer chanted.

SITE: The Transliterated Siddur
URL: siddur.org
NOTES: Scroll down and click on "Table of Contents," then "The Weekday Morning Amidah."

CATEGORY: **Ritual Objects**
SUBJECT: **Aron Kodesh**
EXPLANATION: Explore synagogues around the world to view examples of the *Aron Kodesh*.

SITE: Aron
URL: synagogueart.bizhosting.com/aron.html
NOTES: A picture of an *aron*.

SITE: Congregation Rodfei Zedek Aron Kodesh
URL: www.uscj.org/midwest/chicagorz/aron.html
NOTES: A picture of a modern *aron*.

SITE: Kazimierz, Poland — 'Aron ha Kodesh' (Ark) of Rema Synagogue
URL: www.igc.apc.org/ddickerson/remuh-aron-kodesh.html (see Figure 1-22, opposite)
NOTES: A picture of an old *aron* from a synagogue in Poland.

CATEGORY: **Ritual Objects**
SUBJECT: **Rimmonim**
EXPLANATION: *Rimmonim* are the "crowns" on the Torah.

SITE: Collections — Highlights
URL: www.ncartmuseum.org/collections/highlights/judaic.shtml
NOTES: This museum web site has a number of examples of *rimmonim* from around the world. Click on the link "Click here for more information" to view an enlarged picture.

FIGURE 1-22

SITE: Rimmonim by Simon Harris
URL: www.eclipse.co.uk/exeshul/exeshul/history/rimmonim1.htm
NOTES: A picture of *rimmonim* made by a Jewish silversmith in 1813.

SITE: Rimmonim by Simon Levy
URL: www.eclipse.co.uk/exeshul/exeshul/history/rimmonimlevy.htm
NOTES: A picture of *rimmonim* with the text of their inscription by a Jewish silversmith in 1823.

CATEGORY: Ritual Objects
SUBJECT: Torah Scrolls
EXPLANATION: Compare the different ways Ashkenazic and Sephardic Jews decorate their Torah scrolls.

SITE: Sephardic Torah Scroll
URL: jewishmuseum.net/Permanent/Sephardic.htm
NOTES: Picture and explanation of how a Sephardic Torah scroll differs from an Ashkenazic scroll. Click on the photo to enlarge it.

SITE: Torah
URL: www. uahcweb.org/ny/tinw/ReligiousLiving/ReligiousObjects/
  Torah.htm
NOTES: This site contains numerous pictures and explanations about the Torah scrolls, including the blessings over the reading of the Torah.

SITE: Who? and What? in the Synagogue
URL: scheinerman.net/judaism/synagogue/torah.html
NOTES: This site gives an explanation with diagrams of each of the parts of the Torah scroll and how it is made.

CATEGORY: Ritual Objects
SUBJECT: Wimpel
EXPLANATION: Wimpels are often made by families at the birth of a child and used later for the child's Bar/Bat Mitzvah or wedding. Note that on both of the sites below "wimpel" is spelled incorrectly as "wimple."

SITE: Wimples on the Web
URL: www.uscj.org/metny/huntinhh/wimple.html
NOTES: An explanation of wimpels and how they are used.

SITE: Wimples, Torah Crown, Rimonim
URL: www.jewishmuseum.net/Permanent/Wimples.htm
NOTES: A picture and explanation of Jewish wimpels. Click on the picture for an enlarged view.

CATEGORY: Ritual Objects
SUBJECT: Writing a Sefer Torah
EXPLANATION: Learn how a *sofer* creates a *Sefer Torah*.

SITE: Ask the Sofer
URL: www.stam.net/AskSofer.html (see Figure 1-23, below)
NOTES: On this site, your students can e-mail questions to a *sofer*.

FIGURE 1-23

SITE: Torah
URL: www. uahcweb.org/ny/tinw/ReligiousLiving/ReligiousObjects/
Torah.htm
NOTES: This site has pictures and an explanation of how a *Sefer Torah* is written.

CATEGORY: Texts
SUBJECT: Tanach Selections
EXPLANATION: Many biblical passages relate to Shemini Atzeret and Simchat Torah. These include selections that mention the holiday or explain its themes, as well as the Torah/Haftarah portions associated with the holiday (traditional and Reform). Be sure to explore: Genesis 1:1-2:4, 48:16, 20; Leviticus 23:36; Numbers 29:15, 35-30:1; Deuteronomy 14:22-16:17, 33:1-34:12; Joshua 1:1-18; I Kings 8:54-66.

SITE: Divrei Torah — Commentaries
URL: shamash.org/tanach/dvar.shtml
NOTES: Scroll down for links to dozens of Torah commentary sites.

SITE: Navigating the Bible II
URL: bible.ort.org
NOTES: This site provides English and Hebrew versions of every Torah and Haftarah portion. Under "select language," click on English. On the next page, the "Translation" link will provide the full text in English that can be copied and pasted into a word processing program. The "Torah" and "Haftarot" links display limited sections of the Hebrew text as graphic images. These can be copied by right-clicking on the graphic, selecting "copy," then pasting the graphic into a word processing, page layout, or image editing document.

SITE: World Wide Study Bible
URL: www.ccel.org/wwsb
NOTES: Click on the link to the specific book that you want, then click on the correct chapter from the list of numbers. Scroll down to "More Scriptures" and click on "Jewish Bible." Choose from among the selections. The best English selection is the link "JPS." The "Hebrew" one requires a Hebrew-reading font for your browser. All of these can be cut, pasted, and manipulated in a word processing program. Although the World Wide Study Bible is a Christian site, it has the only easily accessible online Bible text.

CATEGORY: Themes
SUBJECT: Consecration
EXPLANATION: Consecration is a relatively new ritual from the Conservative and Reform movements.

SITE: Reform Judaism
URL: www.rj.org
NOTES: Click on the "Ask the Rabbi" link and e-mail any questions about the ceremony of Consecration.

SITE: United Synagogue of Conservative Judaism
URL: www.uscj.org
NOTES: Click on the link on left bottom of the menu for "Contact Us" and send them an e-mail with your questions.

CATEGORY: Themes
SUBJECT: Parashat HaShavua
EXPLANATION: There are numerous *Parashat HaShavua* study guides on the Internet.

SITE: Weekly Torah Readings
URL: www.uscj.org/midwest/milwaukeecbi/jewish2.htm
NOTES: This site contains an explanation of the concept of reading passages from Torah and Haftarah each week, and a listing of all Torah portions and their corresponding Haftarah readings.

Chanukah

CATEGORY: Arts
SUBJECT: Chanukah Music
EXPLANATION: There are many different types of Chanukah music.

> **SITE:** The Jewish Music Home Page
> **URL:** www.jewishmusic.com
> **NOTES:** Click on the link "Audio Library," then "Hanukah." Select either "Hanukah General" or "Hanukah Kids" to sample a number of selections of Chanukah music using Real Audio. Alternately, click on "Recordings" in the left menu bar, then on "Music Search." Type "Chanukah" in the "Keywords:" box. Try different spellings (Hanukkah, Chanuka, etc), or other Chanukah related words (Maccabee, latke, menorah, etc) for more results.

> **SITE:** Zemerl — The Interactive Database of Jewish Song
> **URL:** www.princeton.edu/zemerl
> **NOTES:** Click on the link for "Hannukke" in the "Holiday" category, and select from the choices provided. Many have midi files for listening.

CATEGORY: Arts
SUBJECT: Ma'oz Tzur
EXPLANATION: *"Ma'oz Tzur"* is perhaps the best known of all Chanukah songs.

> **SITE:** Chanukah Songs, Hanukkah and Maoz Tzur
> **URL:** www.joods.nl/~chazzanut/chanukah.html
> **NOTES:** A brief history of this popular Chanukah song.

SITE: The Jewish Music Home Page
URL: www.jewishmusic.com
NOTES: Click on the link "Audio Library," then "Hanukah." Select "Hanukah General," then click on the the link to Maoz Tzur to download a Real Audio clip.

SITE: Zemerl — The Interactive Database of Jewish Song
URL: www.princeton.edu/zemerl
NOTES: Click on the link for "Hannukke" in the "Holiday" category, and select from one of the choices provided. Most have midi files for listening.

CATEGORY: Arts
SUBJECT: Mi Yimalayl
EXPLANATION: *"Mi Yimalayl"* is a very famous Chanukah song.

SITE: The Jewish Music Home Page
URL: www.jewishmusic.com
NOTES: Click on "Recordings" in the left menu bar, then on "Music Search." Type "Mi Yimaleil" in the "Song name:" box. Try different spellings (Mi Y'malel, Mi Y'maleil,) for more results.

SITE: Mi Y'malel — Who Can Retell
URL:
www.davka.org/what/text/liturgies/chanukkah/chanukkah.06.html
NOTES: The words to Mi Y'malel in Hebrew, English, and transliteration.

SITE: Zemerl — The Interactive Database of Jewish Song
URL: www.princeton.edu/zemerl
NOTES: Click on the link for "Hannukke" in the "Holiday" category, and select from the choices provided. Many have midi files for listening.

CATEGORY: Food
SUBJECT: Chanukah Dishes
EXPLANATION: Look up recipes for special Chanukah foods such as *latkes* and *sufganiot*.

> **SITE:** Jewish Food Mailing List Archives
> **URL:** jewishfood-list.com
> **NOTES:** Click on the "Recipes" link in the left menu, then on "Chanukah" for a long list of Chanukah recipes.

> **SITE:** Mimi's Cyber-Kitchen
> **URL:** www.cyber-kitchen.com
> **NOTES:** Click on "Mimi's Recipes," then scroll down to the "Holiday Central" link on the left-hand side. Click on "Hanukkah" and choose from over a dozen links to Chanukah recipes and to other Chanukah sites.

CATEGORY: Historical Ties
SUBJECT: Greek Culture
EXPLANATION: Greek culture, Hellenism, was the prevalent culture in the world at the time of the Maccabean revolt.

> **SITE:** The Ancient Greek World
> **URL:** www.museum.upenn.edu/greek_World (see Figure 1-24, opposite)
> **NOTES:** Explore special sections with pictures and information concerning land and time, daily life, economy, religion and death.

> **SITE:** Department of Greek and Roman Antiquities
> **URL:** http://www.thebritishmuseum.ac.uk/gr/grgall.html
> **NOTES:** This index of galleries at the British Museum has links to over 20 "rooms" with pictures of artifacts and descriptions of ancient Greek life.

FIGURE 1-24

CATEGORY: Maps

SUBJECT: Greek Empire

EXPLANATION: After Alexander the Great died, his vast empire was divided among his generals. The two primary areas were controlled by the Ptolomys, centered in Egypt, and the Seleucids, centered in Syria.

SITE: The Later Seleucids

URL: www.barnsdle.demon.co.uk/hist/sel.html

NOTES: A chronology of the Seleucid rulers from 187 B.C.E. to the Roman takeover of Syria in 89 B.C.E., detailing the Seleucid's self destruction.

SITE: Mapgrkemp.gif

URL: www.aaronc.com/chronpg/chronbib/mapschr/mapgrkemp.gif

NOTES: A map of the empire of Alexander the Great.

CATEGORY: Maps
SUBJECT: Modin
EXPLANATION: Learn about the home of Mattathias and his sons, where the Maccabean revolt started. Notice its location in respect to Jerusalem.

> **SITE:** Israel Map — Map of Israel with roads
> **URL:** www.templebuilders.com/maps/maphtm.htm
> **NOTES:** A very detailed map of Israel showing the location of Modi'in. Take care with the overall site, however, since this is a Christian religious site.

> **SITE:** Modi'in and the Surrounding Area
> **URL:** www.geocities.com/jelbaum/Modiin.html (see Figure 1-25, opposite)
> **NOTES:** The site has an extensive description of the location and history of Modi'in.

CATEGORY: Places
SUBJECT: Second Temple
EXPLANATION: The temple, that was defiled by the Greeks, was the center of the rededication of the Maccabees.

> **SITE:** Jews and Jerusalem — First Temple
> **URL:** judaism.about.com/library/weekly/aa123100b.htm
> **NOTES:** Information about King David and the building of First Temple. Select the link to "Second Temple" for additional information.

> **SITE:** Ritmeyer Archaeological Design
> **URL:** homepage.ntlworld.com/ritmeyer/index.shtml
> **NOTES:** This site contains numerous pictures of what archaeologists believe the Temple looked like. Explore the various links for many photos and much interesting information.

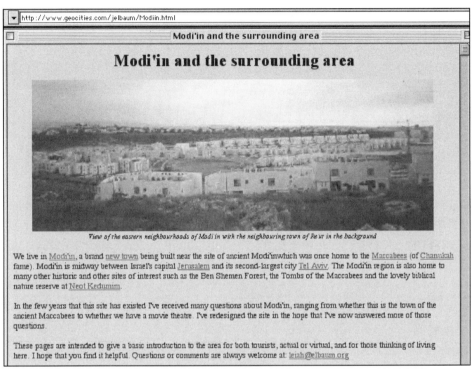

FIGURE 1-25

SITE: The Temple Mount in Jerusalem
URL: www.templemount.org
NOTES: Links to dozens of sites concerning the location, history and descriptions of the Temple Mount.

CATEGORY: Prayers
SUBJECT: Al Hanissim
EXPLANATION: *"Al Hanissim"* is a special prayer that is included in the *"Amidah"* and the *"Birkat HaMazon"* during Chanukah.

SITE: Chanukah — The Festival of Lights
URL: members.aol.com/LazerA/chanukah.htm
NOTES: Scroll down for a short discussion and translation of the prayer.

SITE: The essence of Hanuka

URL: www.jajz-ed.org.il/festivls/hanuka/h2.html

NOTES: This site provides a detailed analysis of this Chanukah prayer.

CATEGORY: Prayers
SUBJECT: Hallel

EXPLANATION: The *Hallel*, recited during Festivals, consists of Psalms 113-118.

SITE: Hallel — "Praise of G-D" — OU.ORG

URL: www.ou.org/chagim/hallel.htm

NOTES: The site includes a detailed explanation of the development of the *Hallel* section and how and when it is recited.

CATEGORY: Ritual Objects
SUBJECT: Chanukiah

EXPLANATION: The *Chanukiah* is the special menorah with nine branches, used only on Chanukah.

SITE: The Chanukah Menorah

URL: www.uahcweb.org/ny/tinw/ReligiousLiving/ReligiousObjects/
Menorah.htm

NOTES: This temple site provides an explanation of the *Chanukiah*, numerous pictures, and the blessings for lighting the Chanukah candles.

SITE: Chanukah On the Net —The Menorah

URL: www.holidays.net/chanukah/menorah.html (see Figure 1-26, opposite)

NOTES: A brief explanation and pictures of the *Chanukiah*.

CATEGORY: Ritual Objects
SUBJECT: Dreidel/Sevivon

EXPLANATION: The *dreidel*, or *sevivon*, is the four sided top that is used on Chanukah.

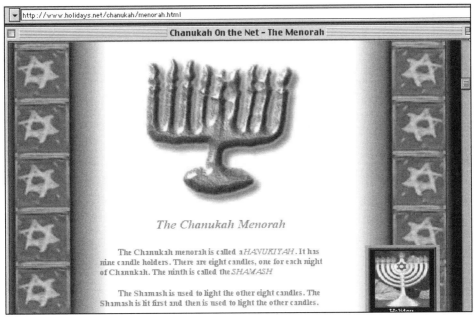

FIGURE 1-26

SITE: Chanukah on the Net — The Dreidle
URL: www.holidays.net/chanukah/dreidel.html (see Figure 1-27, p. 68)
NOTES: Explanation of the *dreidel* and the rules for playing the *dreidle* game.

SITE: ohr.edu — The Secret of the Dreidel
URL: www.ohr.org.il/special/chanukah/chan95.htm
NOTES: A *midrash* on the history of the *dreidel*, linking it to Jewish history.

CATEGORY: Ritual Objects
SUBJECT: Menorah
EXPLANATION: Compare the standard seven-branched menorah with the *Chanukiah*.

FIGURE 1-27

SITE: The Knesset

URL: www.knesset.gov.il

NOTES: This is the official web site of the Knesset in Israel. Click on the "Entrance" link for an English version. Click on the "Knesset Tour" link, and then "The Menorah" for the story and symbolism of the Great Menorah, photos, and a Quick Time movie that you can download.

SITE: The Menorah

URL: www.templeinstitute.org/vessels/menorah.html

NOTES: A short essay on the Temple menorah as described in Exodus. Included is a picture of a menorah that can be enlarged.

CATEGORY: Texts
SUBJECT: Text Selections
EXPLANATION: There are several English and Hebrew texts from the Apocrypha that deal with or relate to Chanukah. Be sure to explore: I Maccabees, II Maccabees, and Judith.

> **SITE:** World Wide Study Bible
> **URL:** www.ccel.org/wwsb
> **NOTES:** Click on the link to the specific book that you want, then click on the correct chapter from the list of numbers. Scroll down to "More Scriptures" and click on "Jewish Bible." Choose from among the selections. The best English selection is the link "JPS." The "Hebrew" one requires a Hebrew-reading font for your browser. All of these can be cut, pasted and manipulated in a word processing program. Although the World Wide Study Bible is a Christian site, it has the only easily accessible online Bible text.

Tu B'Shevat

CATEGORY: Miscellaneous
SUBJECT: Magazines/Newspapers
EXPLANATION: Search for articles and pictures that deal with the themes of Tu B'Shevat.

> **SITE:** Yahoo! News and Media: Magazines
> **URL:** dir.yahoo.com/news_and_media/magazines
> **NOTES:** Select first from the subject you desire, then select from numerous links to magazines around the country. Most of these have online versions of their text. Search through some of them to locate appropriate stories.

> **SITE:** Yahoo! News and Media: Newspapers
> **URL:** dir.yahoo.com/News_and_Media/Newspapers
> **NOTES:** Scroll down to select from dozens of links to newspapers around the country. Most of these have online versions of their complete text. Search through some of them to locate appropriate stories.

CATEGORY: Organizations
SUBJECT: Jewish National Fund
EXPLANATION: In one century, the Jewish National Fund has planted more than 150 million trees in Israel and changed over 265 square miles of what was once swamp or desert into arable land. It is customary to buy trees from the JNF for planting in Israel during Tu B'Shevat.

SITE: JNF Main

URL: www.jnf.org

NOTES: This is the web site for the Jewish National Fund. It gives current information as well as the history of the organization. You can order trees online to be planted in Israel.

CATEGORY: Organizations

SUBJECT: Neot Kedumim

EXPLANATION: Tu B'Shebat is the New Year of the Trees in Israel. Investigate how the goals of this organization relate to the holiday.

SITE: NEOT KEDUMIM Biblical Landscape Reserve in Israel

URL: www.neot-kedumim.org.il (see Figure 1-28, below)

NOTES: This is the web site for Neot Kedumim, the Biblical Landscape Reserve in Israel.

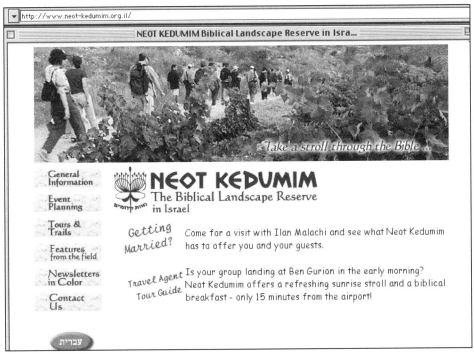

FIGURE 1-28

CATEGORY: Organizations
SUBJECT: Shomrei Adamah
EXPLANATION: Investigate how the goals of this organization relate to Tu B'Shevat.

> **SITE:** Shomrei Adamah
> **URL:** www.geocities.com/guardiansoftheearth/index.html
> **NOTES:** This is the web site for Shomrei Adamah, a non-profit Jewish environmental group in the Washington, D.C. area.

CATEGORY: Texts
SUBJECT: Tanach Selections
EXPLANATION: There are several English and Hebrew texts that deal with or relate to Tu B'Shevat. These include Genesis 1:11-13, 28, 7:3; Leviticus 19:23-25, 26:3-18; Deuteronomy 8:7-8, 20:19; Micah 4:3-4; Proverbs 3:17-18; Psalms 1:3, 65:10-12, 92:13-16, 104, 120-134; and Song of Songs 2:3.

> **SITE:** Divrei Torah – Commentaries
> **URL:** shamash.org/tanach/dvar.shtml
> **NOTES:** Scroll down for links to dozens of Torah commentary sites.

> **SITE:** Navigating the Bible II
> **URL:** bible.ort.org
> **NOTES:** This site provides English and Hebrew versions of every Torah and Haftarah portion. Under "select language" click on English. On the next page, the "Translation" link will provide the full text in English that can be copied and pasted into a word processing program. The "Torah" and "Haftarot" links display limited sections of the Hebrew text as graphic images. These can be copied by right-clicking on the graphic, selecting "copy," then pasting the graphic into a word processing, page layout, or image editing document.

SITE: World Wide Study Bible

URL: www.ccel.org/wwsb

NOTES: Click on the link to the specific book that you want, then click on the correct chapter from the list of numbers. Scroll down to "More Scriptures" and click on "Jewish Bible." Choose from among the selections. The best English selection is the link "JPS." The "Hebrew" one requires a Hebrew-reading font for your browser. All of these can be cut, pasted and manipulated in a word processing program. Although the World Wide Study Bible is a Christian site, it has the only easily accessible online Bible text.

CATEGORY: Themes

SUBJECT: Almonds

EXPLANATION: The almond tree is one of the first trees to bloom in Israel. By Tu B'Shevat, almond trees are in full bloom.

SITE: Almonds Are In! The Almond Board of California

URL: www.almondsarein.com (see Figure 1-29, p. 74)

NOTES: This site has a great deal of information about almonds.

SITE: Nunes Farms — Almonds

URL: www.nunesfarms.com/almonds.htm

NOTES: This commercial site has numerous pictures of almonds. Click on any one of them for a larger view.

CATEGORY: Themes

SUBJECT: Apple

EXPLANATION: The apple symbolizes the splendor of God as seen in Song of Songs 23: "Like an apple tree among the trees of the forest, so is my beloved among the youths . . ."

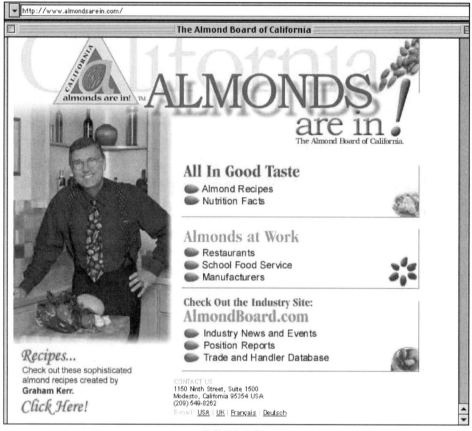

FIGURE 1-29

SITE: America's Fruit Company — Apple Selections
URL: www.thefruitcompany.com/ap_fuji.htm
NOTES: Click on any picture for a description of the characteristics of several varieties of apples. This is a commercial site.

SITE: Apples! Apples!
URL: www.guilford.k12.nc.us/webquests/Apples/apples.htm
NOTES: A teacher web site full of ideas, activities, and information about apples.

SITE: Apple Journal — "A Passion for Apples"
URL: www.applejournal.com
NOTES: This site contains almost everything you would want to know about apples. To view a number of photos of apples, click on the "Gallery" link under "Apple Archive" in the left-side menu. Then click on any of the "page" links in the first paragraph. Click on any photo for an enlarged view.

CATEGORY: Themes
SUBJECT: Charuv/Bokser/Carob
EXPLANATION: The carob is of lowly fare, and accordingly symbolizes humility. It is a fruit often eaten on Tu B'Shevat.

SITE: Carob
URL: www.gilead.net/health/Carob.htm
NOTES: This site provides a great deal of information about carob. Note that this is a Christian Missionary site, although this particular page can be used for the classroom.

SITE: Carob
URL: www.humorscope.com/herbs/carob.html
NOTES: This site provides a brief overview of the history and uses of carob.

SITE: The Products of the Carob Tree
URL: www.alimcarat.com/ve/elaboracion.htm
NOTES: The site contains small pictures of the carob tree and the various products that come it.

CATEGORY: Themes
SUBJECT: Farms
EXPLANATION: Tu B'Shevat celebrates the miracle of planting and growth. Look for pictures of planting, farming, or anything relating to nature or farm life in Israel.

SITE: Farming and Agriculture: Israel Today – Israel My Beloved
URL: www.israelmybeloved.com/today/farming_agriculture
NOTES: Though this is a Christian site, it has excellent information about farming and agriculture in Israel.

SITE: Farm Animals
URL: www.kidsfarm.com/farm.htm (see Figure 1-30, below)
NOTES: Pictures of and information about farm animals.

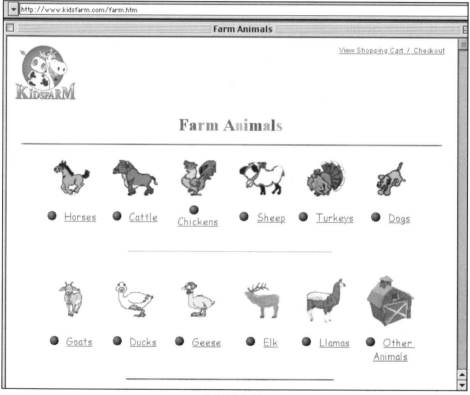

FIGURE 1-30

SITE: Living History Farms; Get Your Grip on History
URL: www.lhf.org
NOTES: Explore farms throughout American history. Click on the links in the "Take a Tour" section near the bottom of the page.

CATEGORY: Themes
SUBJECT: Figs
EXPLANATION: The fig is a symbol of peace.

SITE: Fascinating Fig Facts
URL: www.valleyfig.com/funfacts.htm
NOTES: Lots of information about and pictures of figs.

SITE: History of the Fig
URL: www.valleyfig.com/history.htm
NOTES: This site from a Fresno, California fig grower offers a brief history of figs around the world and in California.

SITE: Home Fruit Production — Figs
URL: aggie-horticulture.tamu.edu/extension/homefruit/fig/fig.html
NOTES: A lot of information about several varieties of figs and how to grow them, as well as a picture.

CATEGORY: Themes
SUBJECT: Rainforests
EXPLANATION: Discuss the implications of the vast destruction of rainforests on the world's ecosystem.

SITE: Rainforest Action Network: Kids' Corner
URL: www.ran.org/kids_action
NOTES: Another Rainforest Action Network site, especially for kids. Included are numerous projects for kids to help save the rainforest.

SITE: Rainforest Field Trip
URL: www.field-guides.com/sci/rainforest/index.htm
NOTES: At this site you can take a virtual field trip to the rainforest.

SITE: World Rainforest Information Portal
URL: www.rainforestweb.org
NOTES: This site from the Rainforest Action Network provides a great deal of of information about rainforests.

CATEGORY: Themes
SUBJECT: Trees
EXPLANATION: Trees are integral to the holiday of Tu B'Shevat. Find pictures of various kinds of trees.

SITE: The Field Trips Site
URL: www.field-guides.com
NOTES: Click on the "virtual field trips" link, then select a virtual field trip in one of the ecosystems offered. Most appropriate: Rainforest, Temperate Forest Biome.

SITE: The Virtual Orchard
URL: www.virtualorchard.net
NOTES: Many links to apple orchards around the country. Most have pictures.

SITE: The World's Biomes
URL: www.ucmp.berkeley.edu/glossary/gloss5/biome (see Figure 1-31, opposite)
NOTES: Select "Forests" and "Grasslands" for information and pictures.

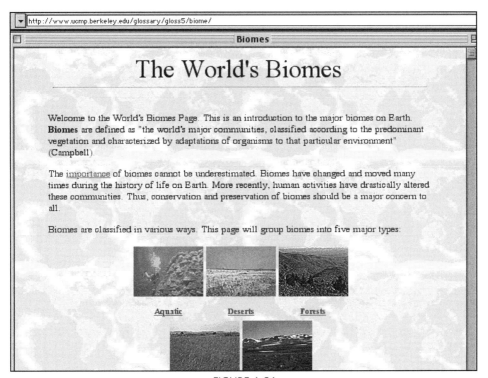

FIGURE 1-31

Purim

CATEGORY: Food
SUBJECT: Purim Dishes
EXPLANATION: Explore recipes for Purim dishes, especially *Hamantashen*.

> **SITE:** Archives of the rec.food.cuisine.jewish Newsgroup
> **URL:** www.cyber-kitchen.com/rfcj/category.cgi?category=PURIM
> **NOTES:** Scroll down and click on "PURIM" for links to dozens of recipes, including 16 different recipes for *hamentaschen*.

> **SITE:** Jewish Food Mailing List Archives
> **URL:** jewishfood-list.com
> **NOTES:** Click on the "Recipes" link in the left menu, then on "Purim" in the list of major topics. Select from over 30 Purim recipes.

> **SITE:** Purim on Mimi's Cyber-Kitchen
> **URL:** www.cyber-kitchen.com/holidays/purim/recipes.htm
> **NOTES:** Choose from eleven holiday recipes.

CATEGORY: Maps
SUBJECT: Persia
EXPLANATION: The Purim story took place in Persia. Explore a map of the ancient Persian empire.

> **SITE:** Persian Empire
> **URL:**
> ancienthistory.about.com/library/bl/bl_maps_asia_persianempire.htm
> **NOTES:** Select from a number of maps of the Persian Empire.

SITE: Persian Empire, 529 B.C.E

URL: ragz-international.com/mapspersiacyrus500.gif

NOTES: A simple map of the Persian Empire.

CATEGORY: Organizations

SUBJECT: Anti-Defamation League

EXPLANATION: The struggle against anti-Semitism is the major theme of Purim. The ADL is the primary Jewish organization that combats acts of anti-Semitism.

SITE: ADL: Fighting Anti-Semitism, Bigotry and Extremism

URL: www.adl.org (see Figure 1-32, below)

NOTES: This is the web site for the B'nai Brith Anti-Defamation League. It includes news and resources on such topics as anti-Semitism, terrorism, religious freedom, civil rights, extremism, and the Holocaust. Explore the many links on the left side and bottom of the main page.

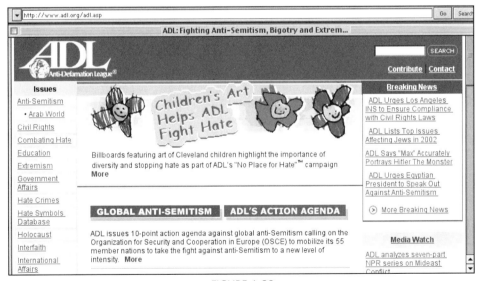

FIGURE 1-32

CATEGORY: Personalities
SUBJECT: Enemies of Israel
EXPLANATION: Look up information on some of the primary enemies of the Jewish people: Antiochus IV (vs. Maccabees, 165 B.C.E.), Torquemada (Grand Inquisitor, Spain, 1492 C.E.), Pharoah (Egypt, c. 1220 B.C.E., possibly Ramses — look him up), Czar Nicholas I (early nineteenth century Russia), Hitler (twentieth century Germany), Saddam Hussein (leader of Iraq in the twentieth and early twenty-first century).

> **SITE:** Biography
> **URL:** www.biography.com
> **NOTES:** Use the BioSearch box to locate famous individuals.

> **SITE:** Lives: The Biography Resource
> **URL:** amillionlives.com
> **NOTES:** Under "Individuals," click on the first letter of the last name of the person you wish to research. Then scroll down to find the name you seek.

CATEGORY: Prayers
SUBJECT: Al HaNissim
EXPLANATION: *"Al HaNissim"* is a special prayer that is included in the *"Amidah"* and the *"Birkat HaMazon"* during Purim.

> **SITE:** Ahavat Israel — Purim — Having Fun the Jewish Way
> **URL:** www.ahavat-israel.com/ahavat/torat/purim.asp
> **NOTES:** Scroll down for an explanation and translation of the prayer.

> **SITE:** The Mitzvos of Purim
> **URL:** members.aol.com/LazerA/purim.htm
> **NOTES:** Scroll down for an explanation and translation of the prayer.

CATEGORY: Texts
SUBJECT: Tanach Selections
EXPLANATION: Several biblical passages relate to Purim. These include selections that mention or explain the themes of the holiday, as well as the Torah/Haftarah portions associated with the holiday (traditional and Reform). Be sure to explore: Exodus 17; The Book of Esther.

SITE: Divrei Torah – Commentaries
URL: shamash.org/tanach/dvar.shtml
NOTES: Scroll down for links to dozens of Torah commentary sites.

SITE: Navigating the Bible II
URL: bible.ort.org
NOTES: This site provides English and Hebrew versions of every Torah and Haftarah portion. Under "select language" click on English. On the next page, the "Translation" link will provide the full text in English that can be copied and pasted into a word processing program. The "Torah" and "Haftarot" links display limited sections of the Hebrew text as graphic images. These can be copied by right-clicking on the graphic, selecting "copy," then pasting the graphic into a word processing, page layout, or image editing document.

SITE: World Wide Study Bible
URL: www.ccel.org/wwsb
NOTES: Click on the link to the specific book that you want, then click on the correct chapter from the list of numbers. Scroll down to "More Scriptures" and click on "Jewish Bible." Choose from among the selections. The best English selection is the link "JPS." The "Hebrew" one requires a Hebrew-reading font for your browser. All of these can be cut, pasted and manipulated in a word processing program. Although the World Wide Study Bible is a Christian site, it has the only easily accessible online Bible text.

CATEGORY: Themes
SUBJECT: Gragger
EXPLANATION: The gragger is a noisemaker, used to blot out the name of Haman whenever heard during the reading of the Scroll of Esther.

> **SITE:** All Judaica
> **URL:** www.alljudaica.com
> **NOTES:** In the search box, type in "groggers" (note the spelling — it must be spelled this way). Click "Go". You'll see a number of links to unusual graggers. Many photos can be enlarged by clicking on them.

> **SITE:** JudaicaStore.com
> **URL:** www.judaicany.com/holidays.shtml#purim
> **NOTES:** Click on the link for "Groggers." You'll be provided with a number of pictures of various graggers. Click on any picture to enlarge it.

> **SITE:** Purim on the Net — Gragger
> **URL:** www.holidays.net/purim/gragger.html (see Figure 1-33, opposite)
> **NOTES:** Information about graggers and how to make your own.

CATEGORY: Themes
SUBJECT: Masks
EXPLANATION: Wearing masks is part of the joyous celebration of this holiday.

> **SITE:** Costume Madness — Aish Purim Site
> **URL:** www.aish.com/holidays/purim/costume_madness.asp
> **NOTES:** This site gives the history of dressing up in costume and wearing masks to conceal one's identity at Purim.

> **SITE:** Mardi Gras Zone
> **URL:** www.mardigraszone.com/retail/default.php
> **NOTES:** Click "Dress up" in the left menu examples of some of the most unusual masks you've ever seen. Click on any photo to enlarge.

FIGURE 1-33

SITE: Purim on the Net — Costumes
URL: www.holidays.net/purim/costumes.html (see Figure 1-34, p. 86)
NOTES: Information about and examples of Purim masks.

CATEGORY: Themes
SUBJECT: Tzedakah
EXPLANATION: Giving *mishloach manot*, a form of *tzedakkah*, is a Purim custom.

SITE: Volunteer Match
URL: www.volunteermatch.org
NOTES: Under "Find" enter your zip code and click "go." Then use the pull-down menus to specify how far you are willing to travel and what type of volunteer work you would like to do. Click "go" and choose from among the links presented, which include contact information.

FIGURE 1-34

SITE: Ziv Tzedakah Fund

URL: www.ziv.org (see Figure 1-35, opposite)

NOTES: Danny Siegel's *tzedakah* site includes a wealth of information and ideas for doing *mitzvot*. Scroll to the very bottom of the page and click on "116 Mitzvah Suggestions" for ideas.

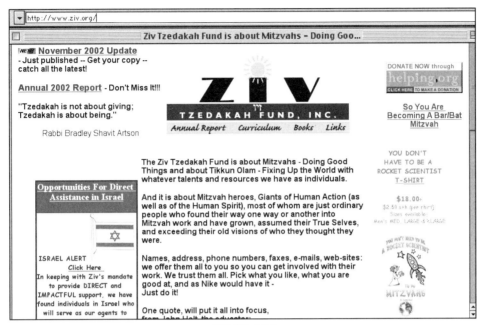

FIGURE 1-35

Pesach

CATEGORY: Arts
SUBJECT: Adir Hu
EXPLANATION: *"Adir Hu"* is a well-known Pesach song sung near the end of the *seder*.

> **SITE:** The Jewish Music Home Page
> **URL:** www.jewishmusic.com
> **NOTES:** Click on "Audio Library" in the top menu, then on "Passover." You will be provided with links to several clips of Passover songs that you can listen to using Real Audio. Alternately, click on "Recordings" in the left menu bar, then on "Music Search." Type "Adir Hu" in the "Song name:" box, then click "Submit." You will see a number of recordings containing a version of the song, several of which have sound clips for listening.

CATEGORY: Arts
SUBJECT: Chad Gadya
EXPLANATION: *"Chad Gadya"* is one of the best known and most delightful songs of Pesach, sung near the end of the *Seder*.

> **SITE:** The Jewish Music Home Page
> **URL:** www.jewishmusic.com
> **NOTES:** Click on "Audio Library" in the top menu, then on "Passover." You will be provided with links to several clips of Passover songs that you can listen to using Real Audio. Alternately, click on "Recordings" in the left menu bar, then on "Music Search." Type "Chad Gadya" in the "Song name:" box, then click "Submit." You will see a number of recordings containing a version of the song, several of which have sound clips for listening.

SITE: Nurit Reshef: Music Room Pesach
URL: www.bus.ualberta.ca/yreshef/pesach/musicroom.html (see Figure 1-36, below)
NOTES: Click on "Midi Room"; select the "Had-Gad-Ya" from the pull-down menu, and click "Play It!" You can follow along with the words as you listen.

FIGURE 1-36

CATEGORY: Arts
SUBJECT: Echad Mi Yodea
EXPLANATION: *"Echad Mi Yodea"* is one of the most famous and enjoyable songs of Pesach, sung near the end of the *Seder*.

SITE: Echad
URL: jnul.huji.ac.il/dl/music/passover/
NOTES: This site contains links to 12 different versions of the popular Pesach song. Click on any of them to download a sound file.

SITE: The Jewish Music Home Page
URL: www.jewishmusic.com
NOTES: Click on "Audio Library" in the top menu, then on "Passover." You will be provided with links to several clips of Passover songs that you can listen to using Real Audio. Alternately, click on "Recordings" in the left menu bar, then on "Music Search." Type "Echad Mi Yodea" in the "Song name:" box, then click "Submit." There may be no sound clips currently posted for this song, but additional links are always being added. You might also try alternate spellings, such as *"Echod Mi Yodea."*

SITE: Nurit Reshef: Music Room Pesach
URL: www.bus.ualberta.ca/yreshef/pesach/musicroom.html
NOTES: Click on "Midi Room"; select the song from the pull-down menu, and click "Play it!" You can follow along with the words as you listen.

CATEGORY: Arts
SUBJECT: Pesach Music
EXPLANATION: There are many types of Pesach music recorded.

SITE: The Jewish Music Home Page
URL: www.jewishmusic.com
NOTES: Click on the link "Audio Library," then "Passover." You can sample a number of selections of Passover music and listen to sound clips using Real Audio.

SITE: Zemerl — The Interactive Database of Jewish Song
URL: www.princeton.edu/zemerl
NOTES: Click on the link for "Pesakh" in the "Holiday" category; then choose from the song titles in the left column. Many have sound clips that can be downloaded for listening.

CATEGORY: Food

SUBJECT: Kosher L'Pesach

EXPLANATION: There are many very specific laws regarding foods being Kosher for Pesach.

SITE: Kashrut.Com

URL: www.kashrut.com (see Figure 1-37, below)

NOTES: One of the premier sites for finding out about everything kosher. Click on the "PASSOVER" link in the top menu bar.

FIGURE 1-37

SITE: Kosher for Passover

URL: www.kosher4passover.com

NOTES: A very comprehensive site for learning about what is kosher for Passover. Be sure to explore the links "Passover Shopping," "Passover Guides," and "Koshering Your Home."

CATEGORY: Food

SUBJECT: Matzah

EXPLANATION: Explore how *matzah* is made.

> **SITE:** CNN — Making Matzah a Passover Tradition
> **URL:** www.cnn.com/EVENTS/world_of_faith/9604/04/israel_leaven/
> index.html (see Figure 1-38, below)
> **NOTES:** Everything you want to know about making *matzah*.
> Includes a number of links to other interesting sites.

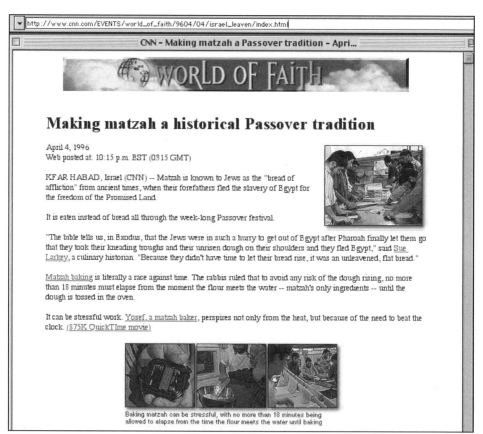

FIGURE 1-38

SITE: Passover Clipart: Matzo — Graphic Design

URL: graphicdesign.miningco.com/arts/graphicdesign/library/
passover/blpasclip1.htm

NOTES: A number of clip art pictures of *matzah*, and instructions for copying and saving the images.

CATEGORY: Food
SUBJECT: Pesach Dishes
EXPLANATION: Locate recipes for various types of Pesach foods.

SITE: Jewish Food Mailing List Archives

URL: jewishfood-list.com

NOTES: Click on the "Recipes" link in the left column, then scroll down and click on "Pesach." Choose from any of the categories for dozens of Passover recipes, including 35 different kinds of *charoset*.

SITE: Mimi's Cyber-Kitchen

URL: www.cyber-kitchen.com

NOTES: Click on "Mimi's Recipes," then scroll down to the "Holiday Central" link on the left-hand side. Click on "Passover," then on "Mimi's Passover Recipes," and choose from nearly 30 links to Pesach recipes.

CATEGORY: Maps
SUBJECT: Ancient Egypt
EXPLANATION: Explore a map to see where the Israelites were lived at the time of the Exodus (Goshen) and how they escaped.

SITE: Bible Maps of Bible Times and Lands

URL: www.bible.ca/maps/maps-the-exodus.htm

NOTES: A map showing the possible route of the Exodus. Note that this is a Christian site.

SITE: World.jpg

URL: www.khouse.org/blueletter/images/maps/Otest/world.jpg

NOTES: An ancient map of Egypt and the Middle East is provided.

CATEGORY: Maps
SUBJECT: Israel — Ancient
EXPLANATION: Pesach was one of the pilgrimage festivals. At this time, the Israelites would travel to Jerusalem to offer sacrifices at the Temple. Locate Jerusalem on a map of Israel.

> **SITE:** Bible Maps of Bible Times and Lands
> **URL:** www.bible.ca/maps
> **NOTES:** Choose from among several maps of ancient Israel. Note that this is a Christian site.

> **SITE:** The Hebrews: The Major Cities and Regions
> **URL:** www.wsu.edu/~dee/HEBREWS/ANISRMAP.HTM
> **NOTES:** This is a map of the major biblical cities and regions of ancient Israel.

CATEGORY: Miscellaneous
SUBJECT: Uncle Eli's Haggadah
EXPLANATION: Explore a humorous version of the *Haggadah*, written in the style of Dr. Seuss.

> **SITE:** Uncle Eli's Haggadah
> **URL:** www.ucalgary.ca/~elsegal/Uncle_Eli/Eli.html (see Figure 1-39, opposite)
> **NOTES:** A very entertaining online *Haggadah* that makes one wonder what the world would have been like if Dr. Seuss was Jewish. Click on the links on the left for various parts of the *Seder*.

CATEGORY: Prayers
SUBJECT: Hallel
EXPLANATION: The *"Hallel,"* recited during Festivals, consists of Psalms 113-118.

FIGURE 1-39

SITE: Hallel
URL: www.vbm-torah.org/pesach/hallel.htm
NOTES: This site includes a detailed explanation of why the *"Hallel"* recited on Pesach night is different from all other versions.

SITE: Hallel — "Praise of G-D" — OU.ORG
URL: www.ou.org/chagim/hallel.htm
NOTES: The site includes a detailed explanation of the development of the *"Hallel"* section of the *Siddur* and how and when it is recited.

CATEGORY: Prayers
SUBJECT: Yizkor
EXPLANATION: Yizkor is the memorial service held on the last day of Pesach, as well as the last days of other Festivals and on Yom Kippur.

SITE: Guide to the Jewish Funeral
URL: www.jewish-funerals.org/brochure.htm
NOTES: Information about all aspects of the Jewish funeral and Jewish burial practices.

SITE: Yizkor — Remembrance of the Departed
URL: www.yahrzeit.org/yizkor.html
NOTES: An entire site devoted to Yizkor. Choose from the many links on the side or bottom for a wealth of information on Yizkor practices.

CATEGORY: Ritual Objects
SUBJECT: Haggadah
EXPLANATION: *Haggadot* have been illustrated and written in elaborate forms throughout the centuries.

SITE: History of the Haggadah
URL: www.ohr.org.il/special/pesach/hagghist.htm
NOTES: The site provides a short history of the development of the *Haggadah*.

SITE: Passover
URL: www.israelshop1.com/passover.html
NOTES: This commercial site features several examples of *Haggadot*. Click on the link to "Passover Haggadot" to view a number of covers, and click on any thumbnail to enlarge the photo.

SITE: Passover.net

URL: www.passover.net

NOTES: Click on the link to "The Haggadah" on the left. Then select from links to a translation (with commentary) of the entire *Haggadah*, commentaries, and *midrashim*. Although this site is sponsored by Chabad-Lubavitch, teachers of all denominations can choose what would be appropriate for their classroom curriculum.

CATEGORY: Ritual Objects

SUBJECT: Seder Plates

EXPLANATION: Explore various types of *Seder* plates.

SITE: Seder Plate

URL: uahc.org/ny/tinw/ReligiousLiving/ReligiousObjects/
SederPlate.htm (see Figure 1-40, below)

NOTES: This site provides an explanation of the *Seder* plate as well as numerous pictures.

FIGURE 1-40

SITE: Seder Plates
URL: collections.ic.gc.ca/art_context/statsad.htm
NOTES: This Canadian museum site shows a number of different *Seder* plates. Click on any of the pictures for an enlarged view.

SITE: Virtual Seder Plate
URL: uahc.org/congs/nj/nj006/seder/plate.html
NOTES: Click on any section of the large seder plate for an explanation of that particular Pesach symbol.

CATEGORY: Texts
SUBJECT: Tanach Selections
EXPLANATION: Numerous passages from the Bible deal with or relate to Pesach. These include selections that mention or explore the themes of the holiday, as well as the proper Torah/Haftarah portions (traditional and Reform). Be sure to explore: Exodus 7:14-12:51, 13:8, 14, 16:22, 33:12-34:26; Leviticus 22:26-23:44; Numbers 9:9-13, 28:19-25; Deuteronomy 6:20, 26:5, 29:13-14; Joshua 5:2-6:1, II Kings 23:1-9, 21-25, Ezekiel 37:1-14.

SITE: Divrei Torah — Commentaries
URL: shamash.org/tanach/dvar.shtml
NOTES: Scroll down for links to dozens of Torah commentary sites.

SITE: Navigating the Bible II
URL: bible.ort.org
NOTES: This site provides English and Hebrew versions of every Torah and Haftarah portion. Under "select language" click on English. On the next page, the "Translation" link will provide the full text in English that can be copied and pasted into a word processing program. The "Torah" and "Haftarot" links display limited sections of the Hebrew text as graphic images. These can be copied by right-clicking on the graphic, selecting "copy," then pasting the graphic into a word processing, page layout, or image editing document.

SITE: World Wide Study Bible

URL: www.ccel.org/wwsb

NOTES: Click on the link to the specific book that you want, then click on the correct chapter from the list of numbers. Scroll down to "More Scriptures" and click on "Jewish Bible." Choose from among the selections. The best English selection is the link "JPS." The "Hebrew" one requires a Hebrew reading font for your browser. All of these can be cut, pasted, and manipulated in a word processing program. Although the World Wide Study Bible is a Christian site, it has the only easily accessible online Bible text.

CATEGORY: Themes

SUBJECT: Barley

EXPLANATION: Barley is the grain that is used for the counting of the *omer*. This counting begins on the second day of Pesach.

SITE: Cook's Thesaurus; Barley

URL: www.foodsubs.com/GrainBarley.html

NOTES: Information on several varieties of barley, including photos.

SITE: Digital Images 1 — Barley

URL: www.mhbgallery.com/page7.html

NOTES: Click on the thumbnail photo of a stalk of barley for a larger image.

SITE: Herbal Information Center — Barley Grass: Herbs

URL: www.kcweb.com/herb/barley.htm

NOTES: A brief article about the importance of barley and how it is used.

CATEGORY: Themes

SUBJECT: Kittel

EXPLANATION: A *kittel* is a white robe, usually made of linen, that is worn on Rosh Hashanah, Yom Kippur, and Pesach. It is worn on Pesach to symbolize the release from bondage and slavery and the beginning of a life of freedom.

SITE: Ahavat Israel — Yom Kippur
URL: www.ahavat-israel.com/ahavat/torat/yomkippur.asp
NOTES: Scroll down to the "White Garment" section for a description of the use of the *kittel* on Yom Kippur.

CATEGORY: Themes
SUBJECT: Soviet Jewry
EXPLANATION: The symbolism of the plight of Jews in the former Soviet Union, and now Russia, is often discussed during the *Seder.*

SITE: Ani Yehudi.org
URL: www.aniyehudi.org
NOTES: This site provides religious articles — transliterated prayer books, printable texts, Jewish links, reference information, and more — for Jews of the former Soviet Union.

SITE: NCSJ: National Council on Soviet Jews
URL: www.ncsj.org
NOTES: Country by country report on the status of Jews in the former Soviet Union. The site also includes pictures.

SITE: UCSJ: Union of Councils for Jews in the Former Soviet Union
URL: www.ucsj.org
NOTES: The site for daily news, opinion, and advocacy on Jews and human rights in the former Soviet Union.

Yom HaShoah

CATEGORY: Arts
SUBJECT: Ani Ma'amin
EXPLANATION: Listen to different versions of the most famous Holocaust song, *"Ani Ma'Amin."*

> **SITE:** The Jewish Music Home Page
> **URL:** www.jewishmusic.com
> **NOTES:** Click on "Recordings" in the left menu bar, then on "Music Search." Type "Ani Ma'amin" in the "Song name:" box and click "Submit." You'll see links to several recordings that contain the song, and at least two of them have sound clips that you can download and hear using Real Audio.

> **SITE:** Zemerl — The Interactive Database of Jewish Song
> **URL:** www.princeton.edu/zemerl
> **NOTES:** Click on the "Holocaust" link, then on "Ani Ma'amin" in the list of songs. The page gives some background on the song, but no sound clip is currently available.

CATEGORY: Arts
SUBJECT: Music of the Holocaust
EXPLANATION: Investigate different types of music that was produced during or commemorates the Holocaust.

> **SITE:** The Jewish Music Home Page
> **URL:** www.jewishmusic.com
> **NOTES:** Click on "Audio Library," then on the "Holocaust" link. You can listen to a number of clips of Holocaust music using Real Audio.

SITE: Music of the Holocaust
URL: fcit.usf.edu/holocaust/arts/music.htm (see Figure 1-41, below)
NOTES: This site has links to such topics as Music of the Ghettos and Camps, Music of the Third Reich, "Degenerate" Music, and Music in Response To the Holocaust.

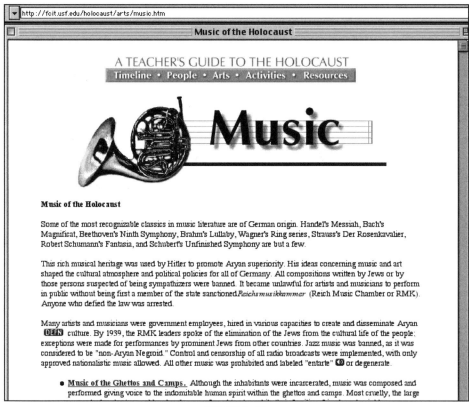

FIGURE 1-41

SITE: Zemerl — The Interactive Database of Jewish Song
URL: www.princeton.edu/zemerl
NOTES: Click on the "Holocaust" link for a list of songs. Some of them have links to downloadable sound clips.

CATEGORY: Maps
SUBJECT: Europe — World War Two
EXPLANATION: Explore a map of Europe to see where the events of the Holocaust took place.

SITE: Historical Atlas of the 20th Century
URL: users.erols.com/mwhite28/20centry.htm (see Figure 1-42, below)
NOTES: Numerous maps, many interactive, of events in the twentieth century. Follow the detailed instructions for how to locate and use the maps in which you are interested.

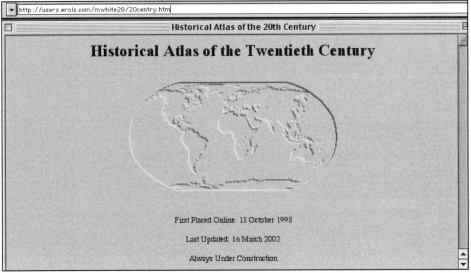

http://users.erols.com/mwhite28/20centry.htm

Historical Atlas of the 20th Century

Historical Atlas of the Twentieth Century

First Placed Online: 18 October 1998

Last Updated: 16 March 2002

Always Under Construction

FIGURE 1-42

SITE: UT Library Online — Perry-Castaneda Map Collection
URL:
www.lib.utexas.edu/maps/historical/history_ww2.html#European
NOTES: A number of World War II maps of various locations in Europe.

CATEGORY: Maps
SUBJECT: Jerusalem — Modern
EXPLANATION: Use these maps to locate Yad Vashem — Har HaZikaron.

> **SITE:** The First Printable Maps of Jerusalem and Tel Aviv on the Internet
> **URL:** www.geocities.com/TheTropics/Beach/5263
> **NOTES:** Maps that can be downloaded and viewed with Adobe Acrobat.

> **SITE:** Jerusalem
> **URL:** www.lib.utexas.edu/maps/world_cities/jerusalem_93.jpg
> **NOTES:** A detailed, easy to read map of Jerusalem's neighborhoods.

CATEGORY: Organizations
SUBJECT: Righteous Gentiles
EXPLANATION: There were thousands of non-Jews who saved and helped Jews during the Holocaust.

> **SITE:** The Jewish Foundation for the Righteous
> **URL:** www.jfr.org
> **NOTES:** The Jewish Foundation of the Righteous is an organization that cares for over a thousand righteous gentiles who rescued Jews during the Holocaust. Click on "Stories of Moral Courage" to read profiles of some of these courageous people.

CATEGORY: Organizations
SUBJECT: Survivors of The Shoah Visual History Foundation
EXPLANATION: In 1994, after filming *Schindler's List,* Steven Spielberg established the Survivors of the Shoah Visual History Foundation in order to videotape and preserve the testimonies of Holocaust survivors and witnesses.

SITE: Survivors of the Shoah Visual History Foundation
URL: www.vhf.org
NOTES: Enter the site, then click on "The Organization" and "The Archive" to read about the work of the Foundation.

CATEGORY: Places
SUBJECT: Kibbutz Lochamay Hagetaot
EXPLANATION: The "Kibbutz of the Ghetto Fighters," located near Haifa, was founded in 1949 by survivors of the Polish and Lithuanian ghettos.

SITE: American Friends of the Ghetto Fighters' House
URL: www.friendsofgfh.org (see Figure 1-43, below)
NOTES: Lots of information about the Ghetto Fighters' Museum, located at Kibbutz Lochamay Hagetaot in Israel. Read about the exhibits and the educational work of the organization. *Yad Layeled* Children's Museum is located at the same site (see below).

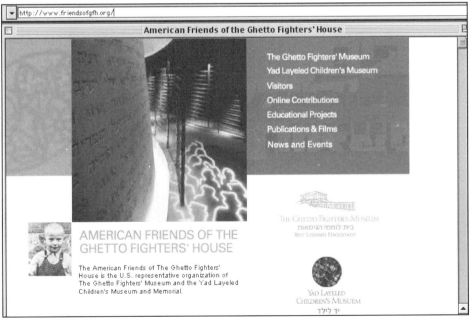

FIGURE 1-43

SITE: Yad Layeled
URL: www.gfh.org.il/english/yad/toc.htm
NOTES: *Yad Layeled* Children's Museum is a living memorial to the Jewish children who perished in the Holocaust. It is located adjacent to the Ghetto Fighters' Museum at Kibbutz Lochamay Hagetaot in Israel. The site features a great deal of information about the museum, as well as links to the Ghetto Fighters' Museum.

CATEGORY: Places
SUBJECT: Kibbutz Yad Mordecai
EXPLANATION: The "kibbutz of the Memorial to Mordecai" is near Ashkelon. It was founded in 1943 and named after Mordecai Anielewicz, the commander of the Warsaw Ghetto uprising.

SITE: Mordecai Anielewicz
URL: www.us-israel.org/jsource/biography/Anielevich.html
NOTES: A biography of the man for whom Yad Mordecai was named, from the Jewish Virtual Library. Click on the links to read more about the Warsaw Ghetto uprising.

CATEGORY: Places
SUBJECT: United States Holocaust Memorial Museum
EXPLANATION: The United States Holocaust Memorial Museum is the newest addition to the Smithsonian Institute in Washington, D.C.

SITE: United States Holocaust Memorial Museum
URL: www.ushmm.org
NOTES: This is the official web site for the museum. Much of the collection and information about the museum is accessible.

CATEGORY: Places
SUBJECT: Yad Vashem
EXPLANATION: Yad Vashem, located on Mount Herzl in Jerusalem, is the best known of all Holocaust museums and memorials.

SITE: Yad Vashem — The Holocaust Martyrs' and Heroes' Remembrance Authority
URL: www.yad-vashem.org.il
NOTES: This is the official web site for Yad Vashem. It contains information about the museum, the Holocaust, and a special link to "On-Line Exhibitions."

CATEGORY: Themes
SUBJECT: Holocaust Stamps
EXPLANATION: Explore commemorative Holocaust stamps produced by the United States Postal Service.

SITE: Teaching the Holocaust through Stamps
URL: mofetsrv.mofet.macam98.ac.il/~ochayo/einvert.htm
NOTES: This web site teaches about the Holocaust through the use of stamps, pictures, children's paintings, text, and photographs. Included are photos of many stamps from around the world that feature Holocaust themes.

Yom HaZikaron

CATEGORY: Themes
SUBJECT: Israel Defense Forces
EXPLANATION: Learn about the history of the Israel Defense Forces.

SITE: IDF History
URL: www.idf.il/english/history/history.stm (see Figure 1-44, below)
NOTES: Many links to the history of the Israeli Defense Forces.
Includes general information, actions in all wars, humanitarian operations, and more.

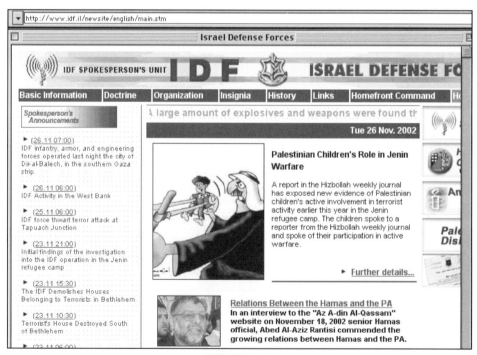

FIGURE 1-44

CATEGORY: Themes
SUBJECT: War of Independence — 1948
EXPLANATION: Learn about Israel's War of Independence.

SITE: Arab-Israeli Conflict in Maps
URL: www.jajz-ed.org.il/100/maps/index.html (see Figure 1-45, below)
NOTES: This site contains links to maps and information about every significant Arab-Israeli conflict, including the 1948 War of Independence. See in particular "The Arab Invasion 1948" and "Armistice Agreements 1949."

FIGURE 1-45

SITE: Israel Defense Forces
URL: www.idf.il/english/history/independance.stm
NOTES: On this page of the Israeli Defense Forces web site, you will find links to the various operations, battles and events of the War of Independence. Each contains a fascinating narrative with photos.

SITE: Israeli War of Independence
URL: www.adl.org/ISRAEL/Record/48war.asp
NOTES: A short article about the war from the ADL web site.

CATEGORY: Themes
SUBJECT: Sinai Campaign — 1956
EXPLANATION: Israel's second major war was fought in 1956.

SITE: The 1956 Sinai Campaign
URL: www.adl.org/ISRAEL/Record/sinai.asp
NOTES: A brief article on the war from the Anti-Defamation League web site.

SITE: Arab-Israeli Conflict in Maps
URL: www.jajz-ed.org.il/100/maps/index.html
NOTES: This site contains links to maps and information about every significant Arab-Israeli conflict, including the 1956 Sinai Campaign. See in particular "The Sinai Campaign 1956."

SITE: The History Guy: Arab-Israeli Wars: Suez/Sinai War 1956
URL: www.historyguy.com/suez_war_1956.html
NOTES: The site contains a short narrative and numerous links to other sites concerning the 1956 Sinai Campaign.

CATEGORY: Themes
SUBJECT: Six-Day War — 1967
EXPLANATION: The Six Day War established Israel as one of the world's leading military powers, and saw the capture of the Old City of Jerusalem, the Western Wall, and the Temple Mount.

SITE: Arab-Israeli Conflict in Maps
URL: www.jajz-ed.org.il/100/maps/index.html
NOTES: This site contains links to maps and information about every significant Arab-Israeli conflict, including the 1967 Six Day War. See in particular "Position of Arab Forces 1967," "Six Day War — June 1967," and "Cease Fire Lines 1967."

SITE: Israel Defense Forces
URL: www.idf.il/english/history/sixday.stm
NOTES: This Israeli Defense Forces web site features a detailed narrative of the events of the Six Day War.

SITE: The Six Day War
URL: hometown.aol.com/RChera/6daywar.html
NOTES: This student-created web site describes the Six Day War and its importance to us today.

CATEGORY: Themes
SUBJECT: Yom Kippur War — 1973
EXPLANATION: On October 6, 1973 — Yom Kippur morning — Egypt and Syria, backed by Iraq and Jordan, launched a surprise attack on Israel.

SITE: The 1973 Yom Kippur War
URL: www.adl.org/ISRAEL/Record/yomkippur.asp
NOTES: A brief article on the war from the Anti-Defamation League web site.

SITE: Arab-Israeli Conflict in Maps
URL: www.jajz-ed.org.il/100/maps/index.html
NOTES: This site contains links to maps and information about every significant Arab-Israeli conflict, including the 1973 Yom Kippur War. See in particular "Egyptian Attack 1973," and "Syrian Attack 1973."

SITE: Yom Kippur War
URL: lexicorient.com/e.o/yomkipwr.htm
NOTES: The site contains a map, time line, explanations, and links to information about the war.

CATEGORY: Places
SUBJECT: Mount Herzl
EXPLANATION: Mount Herzl is the location of the national Israeli cemetery.

SITE: Find a Grave
URL: findagrave.com (see Figure 1-46, below)
NOTES: Use this site to locate the burial place of famous personalities. Go to "Search by location," scroll down to "Asia," then select "Israel." Choose from several personalities and click on a name to see where they are buried and to view a picture of the grave site.

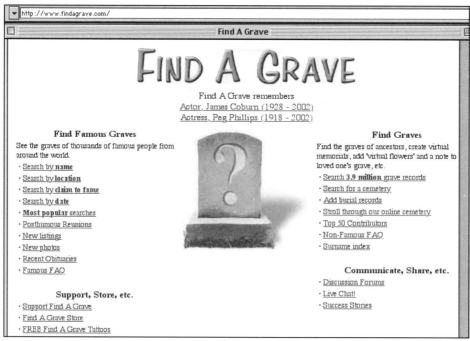

FIGURE 1-46

SITE: Israel Studies — Mount Herzl: The Creation of Israel's National Cemetery

URL: iupjournals.org/israel/iss1-2.html

NOTES: An informational essay about the creation of Israel's National Cemetery. Also included is a biography of Theodor Herzl.

CATEGORY: Texts
SUBJECT: Tanach Selections
EXPLANATION: Psalms 9 and 144 are singled out to read on Yom HaZikaron.

SITE: World Wide Study Bible

URL: www.ccel.org/wwsb

NOTES: Click on the link to the specific book that you want, then click on the correct chapter from the list of numbers. Scroll down to "More Scriptures" and click on "Jewish Bible." Choose from among the selections. The best English selection is the link "JPS." The "Hebrew" one requires a Hebrew reading font for your browser. All of these can be cut, pasted, and manipulated in a word processing program. Although the World Wide Study Bible is a Christian site, it has the only easily accessible online Bible text.

Yom HaAtzma'ut

CATEGORY: Arts
SUBJECT: Hatikvah
EXPLANATION: *"Hatikvah"* is the Israeli national anthem.

SITE: Hatikvah ("The Hope") — Israel's National Anthem
URL: www.stateofisrael.com/anthem (see Figure 1-47, below)
NOTES: This site provides the Hebrew, English translation, and transliteration of *"Hatikvah."* Click on "Listen Now!" to download a sound file.

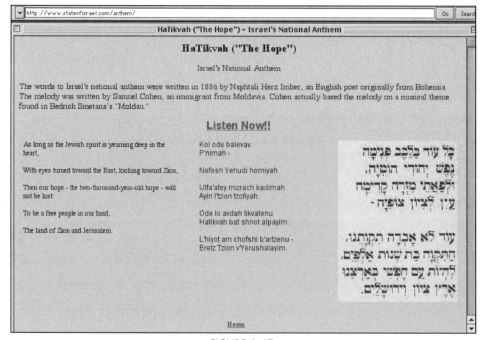

FIGURE 1-47

SITE: The Jewish Music Home Page
URL: www.jewishmusic.com
NOTES: In the left column, click on "Recordings," then on "Music Search." Then type "Hatikvah" in the "Song Name" box and click "Submit." You will be provided with numerous links to recordings that contain a version of this song. Some of them may include a link to hear the song using Real Audio.

SITE: Jewish Music Links
URL: www.haruth.com/JewishMusic.htm
NOTES: Click on the "Hatikvah 1" link to download a version of the song.

CATEGORY: Maps
SUBJECT: Judea
EXPLANATION: Judea was the name of the land of Israel from the time of the Romans. It derived its name from the kingdom of Judah.

SITE: Bible Maps — The Divided Kingdoms 900-722 BC
URL: www.bible.ca/maps/maps-palestine-33AD.htm
NOTES: A simple map of the divided kingdoms of Israel and Judah.

SITE: Canaan/Palestine/Israel
URL: www.mideastweb.org/palmaps.htm
NOTES: Select from a number of maps representing different time periods, including Canaan before the Hebrews, Israel in Early Times, Crusader Palestine, Turkish Palestine, and more.

SITE: Palaestina
URL: www.lib.utexas.edu/maps/historical/palaestina_1849.jpg
NOTES: An ancient map of the region during Roman times.

CATEGORY: Organizations
SUBJECT: World Zionist Organization (W.Z.O.)
EXPLANATION: Founded by Theodor Herzl, the World Zionist Organization is the overall umbrella organization for all Zionist groups in the world.

> **SITE:** Hagshama — Department of the World Zionist Organization
> **URL:** www.wzo.org.il
> **NOTES:** This is the web site of the World Zionist Organization. It contains a great deal of information and links to other sites related to Zionism and Zionist groups.

CATEGORY: Personalities
SUBJECT: Ahad Ha'am
EXPLANATION: Ahad Ha'am (real name Asher Ginzberg) was a great Jewish thinker and exponent of cultural Zionism. His writings had a great influence on those who worked to establish the State of Israel.

> **SITE:** Ahad Ha-am
> **URL:** www.encyclopedia.com/html/A/AhadH1aam.asp
> **NOTES:** A short biography from encyclopedia.com.

> **SITE:** Cultural Zionism
> **URL:** store.yahoo.com/jewish146/polzion1.html
> **NOTES:** A discussion of Ahad Ha'am and the development of Cultural Zionism.

CATEGORY: Personalities
SUBJECT: Menachem Begin
EXPLANATION: A leader of the Irgun, a Prime Minister, and a peacemaker, Menachem Begin was an important figure in Israeli history.

> **SITE:** Menachem Begin
> **URL:** www.ou.org/chagim/yomhaatzmauth/begin.html
> **NOTES:** An extensive but easy to read biography of Menachem Begin.

SITE: Menachem Begin (1913-1992)

URL: www.jajz-ed.org.il/100/people/bios/begin.html (see Figure 1-48, below)

NOTES: A brief biography with pictures.

FIGURE 1-48

CATEGORY: Personalities

SUBJECT: David Ben-Gurion

EXPLANATION: David Ben-Gurion, Israel's first Prime Minister, was a leader in the struggle to establish the State of Israel.

SITE: David Ben-Gurion
URL: www.us-israel.org/jsource/biography/ben_gurion.html
NOTES: A brief biography from the Jewish Virtual Library.

SITE: David Ben-Gurion
URL: www.time.com/time/time100/leaders/index.html
NOTES: A detailed article from a *Time* magazine list of top leaders and revolutionaries who helped define the political and social fabric of our times.

CATEGORY: Personalities
SUBJECT: Eliezer Ben-Yehuda

EXPLANATION: Eliezer Ben-Yehuda is credited with the revival of Hebrew as a modern language, and the eventual establishment of Hebrew as the language of Israel.

SITE: Eliezer Ben-Yehuda and the Revival of Hebrew
URL: www.us-israel.org/jsource/biography/ben_yehuda.html
NOTES: A detailed biography from the Jewish Virtual Library.

SITE: Eliezer Ben Yehuda (1858-1922)
URL: http://www.jajz-ed.org.il/100/people/BIOS/beliezer.html
NOTES: An extensive article about how Ben-Yehuda led the revival of the Hebrew language. A picture is included.

CATEGORY: Personalities
SUBJECT: Chaim Nachman Bialik

EXPLANATION: Chaim Nachman Bialik was a celebrated writer and poet and an important figure in Israeli history.

SITE: Bialik, Haim Nahman (1873-1934)
URL: www.wzo.org.il/home/portrait/bialik.htm
NOTES: A brief biography from The Zionist Exposition.

SITE: Hayyim Nahman Bialik
URL: www.us-israel.org/jsource/biography/bialik.html
NOTES: A brief biography from the Jewish Virtual Library.

CATEGORY: Personalities
SUBJECT: Moshe Dayan
EXPLANATION: Moshe Dayan, an Israeli military warrior who later became a crusader for peace, was an important figure in Israeli history.

SITE: Dayan, Moshe (1915-1981)
URL: www.jajz-ed.org.il/100/people/BIOS/dayan.html
NOTES: A brief overview of Dayan's life and career, with a photograph.

SITE: Moshe Dayan
URL: www.us-israel.org/jsource/biography/Dayan.html
NOTES: A brief biography from the Jewish Virtual Library.

CATEGORY: Personalities
SUBJECT: Theodor Herzl
EXPLANATION: Theodor Herzl is widely considered to be the father of modern political Zionism.

SITE: Jewish Virtual Library: Theodor Herzl
URL: www.us-israel.org/jsource/biography/Herzl.html
NOTES: Information on Herzl's life and career from the American-Israeli Cooperative Enterprise.

SITE: Theodor Herzl (1860-1904)
URL: www.wzo.org.il/home/movement/herzl.htm
NOTES: Click on the "Theodor Herzl" link to view information about the man and his work from this World Zionist Organization site.

CATEGORY: Personalities
SUBJECT: Rav Abraham Isaac Kook
EXPLANATION: Rav Abraham Isaac Kook was a leading thinker and leader of the Religious Zionists. Kook demonstrated that Zionism and traditional Jewish thinking could be compatible.

SITE: Jewish Virtual Library: Rav Kook
URL: www.us-israel.org/jsource/biography/Rav_Kook.html
NOTES: Information on his life from the American-Israeli Cooperative Enterprise.

SITE: Kook, Rabbi Avraham Isaac (1865-1935)
URL: www.wzo.org.il/home/portrait/kook.htm
NOTES: This site provides information on Kook's life and accomplishments, and includes pictures.

CATEGORY: Personalities
SUBJECT: Golda Meir
EXPLANATION: Golda Meir, Israel's third Prime Minister, was a leading socialist Zionist and an important figure in Israeli history.

SITE: Golda Meir (1898-1978) — Israel's Third Prime Minister
URL: www.ou.org/chagim/yomhaatzmauth/golda.html
NOTES: Information from *Collier's Encyclopedia* about Meir's life and career. A photo is included.

SITE: Jewish Virtual Library: Golda Meir
URL: www.us-israel.org/jsource/biography/meir.html
NOTES: Information on Meir's life and career from the American-Israeli Cooperative Enterprise.

CATEGORY: Personalities
SUBJECT: Yitzhak Rabin
EXPLANATION: Yitzhak Rabin was an important Israeli military and political leader. In his later years, Rabin worked to make peace with Israel's Arab neighbors.

SITE: Yitzhak Rabin — Biography
URL: www.nobel.se/peace/laureates/1994/rabin-bio.html
NOTES: A short biography from the Nobel Peace Prize web site.

SITE: Yitzhak Rabin
URL: www.us-israel.org/jsource/biography/rabin.html
NOTES: A brief biography from the Jewish Virtual Library.

CATEGORY: Personalities
SUBJECT: Henrietta Szold
EXPLANATION: Henrietta Szold was the founder of Hadassah, the founder of Youth Aliyah, and a pioneering woman in Zionist politics and affairs.

SITE: Henrietta Szold
URL: www.us-israel.org/jsource/biography/Szold.html
NOTES: An interesting biography from the Jewish Virtual Library.

SITE: Henrietta Szold
URL: search.biography.com/print_record.pl?id=19939
NOTES: A brief biography from Biographies.com

CATEGORY: Personalities
SUBJECT: Chaim Weizmann
EXPLANATION: Chaim Weizmann was a key figure in Israeli history and the first to serve as President of Israel.

SITE: Chaim Weizmann
URL: www.us-israel.org/jsource/biography/weizmann.html (see Figure 1-49, p. 122)
NOTES: A brief biography from the Jewish Virtual Library, including many links to additional information.

SITE: Chaim Weizmann
URL: jewishstudents.net/chaimweizmann.html
NOTES: An informative biography from Jewishpeople.net. Included are a few links to additional sites.

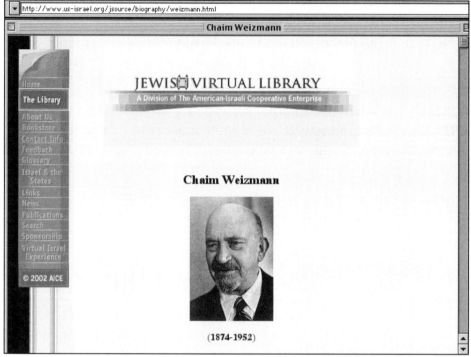

http://www.us-israel.org/jsource/biography/weizmann.html

Chaim Weizmann

JEWISH VIRTUAL LIBRARY
A Division of The American-Israeli Cooperative Enterprise

Home
The Library
About Us
Bookstore
Contact Info
Feedback
Glossary
Israel & the States
Links
News
Publications
Search
Sponsorship
Virtual Israel Experience

© 2002 AICE

Chaim Weizmann

(1874-1952)

FIGURE 1-49

CATEGORY: Places
SUBJECT: Mount of Olives
EXPLANATION: Traditional Jews believe that at the coming of the Messiah, the revival of the dead will begin at the Mount of Olives. It is therefore considered the "ideal spot" for Jews to be buried. When that is not possible, a small bag of soil from that place is sometimes placed in the casket.

SITE: Israel & Jerusalem Photo Album
URL: www.greatcommission.com/israel/Israel.html
NOTES: Scroll down to the "M" section and click on "Mount of Olives Cemeteries" for a full frame photo of the graves covering the hillside. There are also some photos of Christian sites on the Mount in the "Jerusalem" section.

SITE: Israel Slide Show
URL: www.levitt.com/slideshow/slideshow.html
NOTES: Scroll down to the "Mounts" category for a picture of the Mount of Olives. Though this page is part of a Christian site, the pictures are excellent.

SITE: The Jerusalem Archaeological Park
URL: archpark.org.il/index.asp
NOTES: This interactive site allows you to "tour" the western slope of the Mount of Olives. Move your cursor over "Park Map" in the main menu bar and select #5, "The West Slope of the Mount of Olives," from the pull-down menu. Then click on any of the boxed numbers in the right window to view photos and read detailed explanations of the area's major features.

CATEGORY: Themes
SUBJECT: Chalutzim (Pioneers)
EXPLANATION: The *Chalutzim* were the Jewish immigrants to Israel who began to arrive with the First Aliyah in 1882. They were largely responsible for transforming the semi-arid land into what it is today.

SITE: Central Zionist Archives
URL: www.wzo.org.il/cza
NOTES: The archives site for the World Zionist Organization. Click on the "Exhibitions" link for a number of additional links to artifacts that display the work of the *Chalutzim*.

SITE: Focus on Israel — A Voluntary Effort

URL: www.israel.org/mfa/go.asp?MFAH0g7x0

NOTES: Information on the volunteer spirit that drove the building of the State of Israel, and that continues today.

CATEGORY: Themes

SUBJECT: Israel Information

EXPLANATION: These sites are considered the official place on the Internet to locate information about Israel.

SITE: Israel Government Gateway

URL: www.info.gov.il/eng/mainpage.asp

NOTES: This page features dozens of links to information on all aspects of Israel: Economy and Business, Foreign Affairs and Security, Society and Education, Health and Environment, and more.

SITE: The Knesset — the Parliament of Israel

URL: www.knesset.gov.il (see Figure 1-50, opposite)

NOTES: This is the home page for the Knesset. Click on "Entrance" for the English version to take a tour, explore documents, write to members of the Knesset, or research any aspect of the Israeli government.

SITE: Yahoo! Regional: Countries: Israel

URL: dir.yahoo.com/Regional/Countries/Israel

NOTES: On this page you will have access to over 4000 links to other sites containing information about Israel. Categories include Arts and Humanities, Business and Economy, Entertainment, Government, News and Media, Society and Culture, and many more.

CATEGORY: Themes

SUBJECT: Israeli Flag

EXPLANATION: Explore the history and symbolism of the Israeli flag.

FIGURE 1-50

SITE: The Flag and the Emblem
URL: www.israel-mfa.gov.il/mfa/go.asp?MFAH0cph0
NOTES: This site, which is sponsored by Israel's Ministry of Foreign Affairs, features an essay on the history of the Israeli flag.

SITE: Israeli Flags Geographic.org
URL: www.geographic.org/flags/israel_flags.html
NOTES: A simple picture of an Israeli flag. Also included is a photo of an Israeli athlete carrying the flag at the 2000 Olympics.

SITE: The New Israel Shop
URL: www.israelshop1.com
NOTES: Click on the link for "Israeli flags" and select from a variety of sizes, shapes, and designs.

CATEGORY: Themes
SUBJECT: Israeli News
EXPLANATION: Israeli news reports can be read on the Internet.

SITE: Ha'aretz — English
URL: www.haaretzdaily.com
NOTES: This is the English version of one of Israel's major newspapers.

SITE: The Jerusalem Post
URL: www.jpost.com
NOTES: This is the Internet edition of the *The Jerusalem Post*, Israel's major English language paper.

SITE: Kol Israel.com
URL: www.kolisrael.com
NOTES: Kol Israel ("The Voice of Israel") is an Internet news source that provides live radio and news reports from Israel.

SITE: Maariv
URL: www.maariv.co.il
NOTES: This is the online version, in Hebrew, of one of Israel's major newspapers. In order to read the Hebrew, you must have Hebrew fonts installed in your system — visit www.takdinet.co.il/hebrewhelp.shtml for instructions on configuring your browser.

Lag B'Omer

CATEGORY: Maps
SUBJECT: Israel — Modern
EXPLANATION: Look for the locations of Safed and Mount Meron in the Galilee, places that Hasidic Jews visit during Lag B'Omer.

> **SITE:** eMap
> **URL:** www.emap.co.il/NewMezam/MGN/MGNindex_E.htm (see Figure 1-51, p. 128)
> **NOTES:** This site is the Israeli equivalent of Mapquest. Under "Address or starting point" type "Safed" in the "City/Town" box, then click "Locate Address." Use the arrow and zoom buttons on the left to explore the area around Safed and to locate Mount Meron.

> **SITE:** Maps of Israel
> **URL:** www.templebuilders.com/maps/mainindex.htm
> **NOTES:** The site includes several maps of Israel that can be enlarged. Note that this is a Christian religious site.

> **SITE:** Maps of Israel
> **URL:** www.geocities.com/colosseum/loge/7748/maps.html
> **NOTES:** A number of maps of Israel and the Middle East.

CATEGORY: Personalities
SUBJECT: Akiba Ben Joseph (Rabbi Akiva)
EXPLANATION: Rabbi Akiba was a great scholar, patriot, and martyr. A plague broke out among his followers during the period of the Counting of the Omer. It ended suddenly on Lag B'Omer.

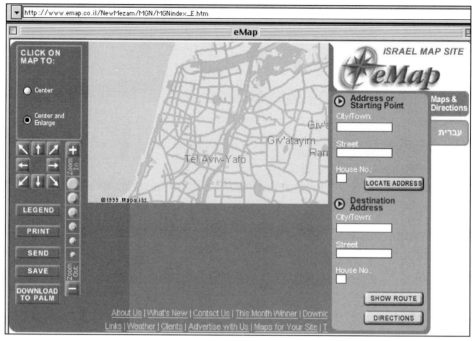

FIGURE 1-51

SITE: Jewish Leaders — Rabbi Akiba
URL: judaism.about.com/library/glossary/bldef-p_akiva.htm
NOTES: A longer biography of Rabbi Akiva.

SITE: Judaism 101: Sages and Scholars
URL: www.jewfaq.org/sages.htm
NOTES: Click on the "Akiba" link for a brief biography.

CATEGORY: Personalities
SUBJECT: Rabbi Shimon Bar Yochai
EXPLANATION: Rabbi Shimon Bar Yochai was a pupil of Rabbi Akiba and a leading scholar in his own right. Escaping from the Romans, Bar Yochai and his son lived in a cave for 13 years. There he supposedly wrote the *Zohar*, the key work of *Kabbalah* (although it is widely considered to have been written by Moses de Leon in thirteenth century Spain).

SITE: Rabbi Shimon Bar Yochai
URL: www.judaicaplus.com/Tzadikim/rashbi.htm
NOTES: A brief biography of Bar Yochai.

SITE: Rabbi Shimon Bar Yochai — Lag B'Omer at OU.ORG
URL: www.ou.org/chagim/lagbaomer/yochai.htm
NOTES: This site contains some basic information about Bar Yochai's life, as well as links to additional information about Lag B'Omer.

CATEGORY: Personalities
SUBJECT: Shimon Bar Kochba
EXPLANATION: Bar Kochba led a revolt against Rome from 132-135 C.E. Rabbi Akiba regarded him as "king messiah."

SITE: The Bar Kochba Rebellion
URL: www.electriciti.com/garstang/judaean/barkochba.htm
NOTES: A brief explanation of the Bar Kochba Revolt, including pictures of coins from that era.

SITE: The Bar-Kokhba Revolt
URL: www.us-israel.org/jsource/Judaism/revolt1.html
NOTES: A lengthy article from the Jewish Virtual Library. Included are a number of additional links.

SITE: Jewish Literacy — Jewish History
URL: www.aish.com/literacy/jewishhistory/
NOTES: Scroll down quite far and click on the link, "Crash Course in Jewish History Part 37 – The Bar Kochba Revolt" for an interesting article.

CATEGORY: Places
SUBJECT: Safed
EXPLANATION: Hasidic Jews typically visit Safed during Lag B'Omer.

SITE: 4 Names — Safed, Safad, Zefat, Tzfat — 1 Town
URL: www.safed.co.il
NOTES: This is the official web site of Safed. Learn all about the city and its history, view photos, and explore numerous other links.

SITE: Ascent of Safed — In The City of Kabbalah
URL: www.ascent.org.il/About/Events/meron.html
NOTES: A description of the events that take place at Mount Meron on Lag B'Omer, with photographs.

SITE: IsraelVisit — SAFED
URL: israelvisit.co.il/safed.htm (see Figure 1-52, opposite)
NOTES: A description of the many ancient sites in Safed.

CATEGORY: Texts
SUBJECT: Tanach Selections
EXPLANATION: Though Lag B'Omer has no biblical roots whatsoever, Leviticus 23:15-16 does relate to the Counting of the Omer.

SITE: Divrei Torah — Commentaries
URL: shamash.org/tanach/dvar.shtml
NOTES: Scroll down for links to dozens of Torah commentary sites.

FIGURE 1-52

SITE: Navigating the Bible II

URL: bible.ort.org

NOTES: This site provides English and Hebrew versions of every Torah and Haftarah portion. Under "Select Language" click on "English." On the next page, the "Translation" link will provide the full text in English that can be copied and pasted into a word processing program. The "Torah" and "Haftarot" links display limited sections of the Hebrew text as graphic images. These can be copied by right-clicking on the graphic, selecting "Copy," then pasting the graphic into a word processing, page layout, or image editing document.

SITE: World Wide Study Bible
URL: www.ccel.org/wwsb
NOTES: Click on the link to the specific book of the Bible that you want, then click on the correct chapter from the list of numbers. Scroll down to "More Scriptures" and click on "Jewish Bible." Choose from among the selections. The best English selection is the link "JPS." The "Hebrew" one requires a Hebrew-reading font for your browser. All of these can be cut, pasted, and manipulated in a word processing program. Although the World Wide Study Bible is a Christian site, it has the only easily accessible online Bible text.

CATEGORY: Themes
SUBJECT: Barley
EXPLANATION: During the Omer, a measure of barley was brought to the Temple each day from Pesach through Shavuot.

SITE: Cook's Thesaurus: Barley
URL: www.foodsubs.com/GrainBarley.html
NOTES: Information on several varieties of barley, including photos.

SITE: Digital Images 1 — Barley
URL: www.mhbgallery.com/page7.html
NOTES: Click on the thumbnail photo of a stalk of barley for a larger image.

SITE: Herbal Information Center — Barley Grass: Herbs
URL: www.kcweb.com/herb/barley.htm
NOTES: A brief article about the importance of barley and how it is used.

CATEGORY: Themes
SUBJECT: Caves
EXPLANATION: During the Bar Kochba Revolt, many Jewish scholars lived in caves to escape the Romans.

SITE: Israel: Man-made caves: Hazan and Luzit

URL: www.wisdom.weizmann.ac.il/~bazlov/israel/hazan.html (see Figure 1-53, below)

NOTES: Pictures and information about the caves that were dug during the Bar Kochba Revolt.

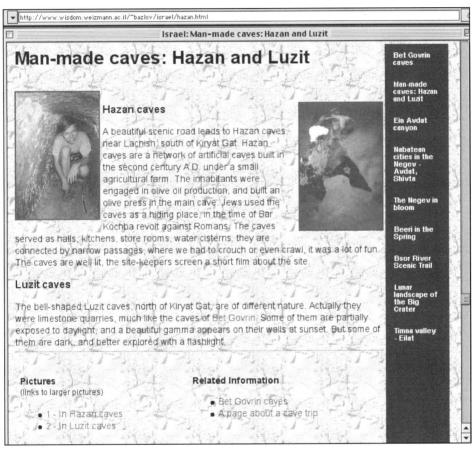

FIGURE 1-53

SITE: Sorek Cave
URL: www.amirmd.com/fam-pic/Sorek.html
NOTES: An interesting page with details about and photographs of a unique cave in Israel. While no rebels hid in this particular cave, it does give an idea of what cave living might have been like.

CATEGORY: Themes
SUBJECT: Kabbalah
EXPLANATION: The *Zohar*, the central portion of *Kabbalah*, was attributed to Rabbi Shimon bar Yochai.

SITE: The Kabbalah Centre
URL: www.Kabbalah.com
NOTES: Lots of explanations and information. Select "Kabbalah on life" to find out what *Kabbalah* teaches on a variety of everyday subjects.

SITE: Kabbalah FAQ
URL: www.digital-brilliance.com/kab/faq.htm
NOTES: A listing of frequently asked questions about *Kabbalah*.

SITE: Kabbalah World Center
URL: www.Kabbalah.info
NOTES: This site contains a great deal of information about *Kabbalah*.

Yom Yerushalayim

CATEGORY: Arts
SUBJECT: Yerushalayim Shel Zahav
EXPLANATION: Listen to a version of one of the most famous songs about Jerusalem.

SITE: Jerusalem of Gold
URL: www.jerusalemofgold.co.il (see Figure 1-54, below)
NOTES: This is an entire web site devoted to the song *"Yerushalayim Shel Zahav."* Included are the history of its writing, the lyrics in Hebrew and English, midi file links, and more.

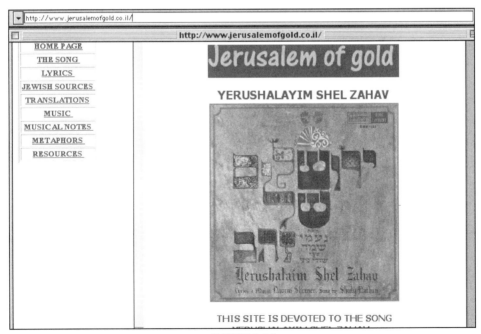

FIGURE 1-54

SITE: The Jewish Music Home Page
URL: www.jewishmusic.com
NOTES: Click on "Recordings" in the left menu bar, then on "Music Search." Type "Yerushalayim Shel Zahav" in the "Song Name:" box, then click "Submit." You will see links to a number of recordings that contain a version of the song. Currently, the only one that contains a sound clip is the last listing, "Very Best Of Israel — Memaitav."

CATEGORY: Maps
SUBJECT: Jerusalem — Modern
EXPLANATION: Explore the various places of interest throughout Jerusalem.

SITE: The First Printable Maps of Jerusalem and Tel Aviv on the Internet
URL: www.geocities.com/TheTropics/Beach/5263
NOTES: Maps that can be downloaded and viewed with Adobe Acrobat.

SITE: Jerusalem
URL: www.lib.utexas.edu/maps/world_cities/jerusalem_93.jpg
NOTES: A detailed, easy to read map of Jerusalem's neighborhoods.

SITE: Jerusalem Map
URL: www.us-israel.org/jsource/History/Jerumap.html
NOTES: A map of Jerusalem and surroundings with major roads.

CATEGORY: Places
SUBJECT: Jerusalem
EXPLANATION: Learn all about the various aspects of Jerusalem.

SITE: Jerusalem Archives
URL: www.jerusalem-archives.org/index1.html
NOTES: Choose any of the links to various time periods. You will find photographs, maps, diagrams, and text that explain Jewish life in Jerusalem during different historical periods, from Ottoman rule through the early days of the State.

SITE: The New Jerusalem Mosaic
URL: jeru.huji.ac.il/open_screen2.htm
NOTES: An extensive site with many excellent links to the history of Jerusalem in various time periods, from the First Temple to the modern State.

SITE: Virtual Israel Experience
URL: www.us-israel.org/jsource/vie/Jerutoc.html
NOTES: Pictures, information, and links to every part of Jerusalem. Select from the many links provided, both within the text and at the bottom of the page.

CATEGORY: Places
SUBJECT: Knesset
EXPLANATION: Learn all about the seat of the Israeli government.

SITE: The Knesset — The Parliament of Israel
URL: www.knesset.gov.il
NOTES: This is the home page for the Knesset. Click on "Entrance" for the English version to take a tour, explore documents, write to Members of the Knesset, or research any aspect of the Israeli government.

CATEGORY: Places
SUBJECT: Kotel
EXPLANATION: Explore a real time picture of the *Kotel* through the Kotel Cam.

SITE: Live Western Wall Camera at Aish HaTorah

URL: www.aish.com/wallcam (see Figure 1-55, below)

NOTES: Get a real time picture of the *Kotel*. Click "Enlarge View" for a full-screen picture.

FIGURE 1-55

SITE: Virtual Israel Experience

URL: www.us-israel.org/jsource/vie/Jerutoc.html

NOTES: Pictures, information, and links to every part of Jerusalem. Select from the many links provided, both within the text and at the bottom of the page.

CATEGORY: Prayers
SUBJECT: Hallel
EXPLANATION: Yom Yerushalayim is a day of special prayers, especially *Hallel*, a collection of joyous Psalms (113-118).

SITE: Hallel — "Praise of G-D" — OU.ORG
URL: www.ou.org/chagim/hallel.htm
NOTES: The site includes a detailed explanation of the development of the *Hallel* section of the *Siddur* and how and when it is recited.

CATEGORY: Themes
SUBJECT: Six Day War — 1967
EXPLANATION: In the 1967 Six Day War, Israel recaptured the Old City of Jerusalem from the Jordanians, ending 19 years of division of the city.

SITE: Arab-Israeli Conflict in Maps
URL: www.jajz-ed.org.il/100/maps/index.html
NOTES: This site contains links to maps and information about every significant Arab-Israeli conflict, including the 1967 Six Day War. See in particular "Position of Arab Forces 1967," "Six Day War — June 1967," and "Cease Fire Lines 1967."

SITE: Israel Defense Forces
URL: www.idf.il/english/history/sixday.stm
NOTES: This Israeli Defense Forces web site features a detailed narrative of the events of the Six Day War.

SITE: Six Days in June
URL: www.israel-mfa.gov.il/mfa/go.asp?MFAH0dy70 (see Figure 1-56, p. 140)
NOTES: This site from Israel's Ministry of Foreign Affairs gives a detailed account of the 1967 Six Day War.

SITE: The Six Day War
URL: hometown.aol.com/RChera/6daywar.html
NOTES: This student-created web site describes the Six Day War and its importance to us today.

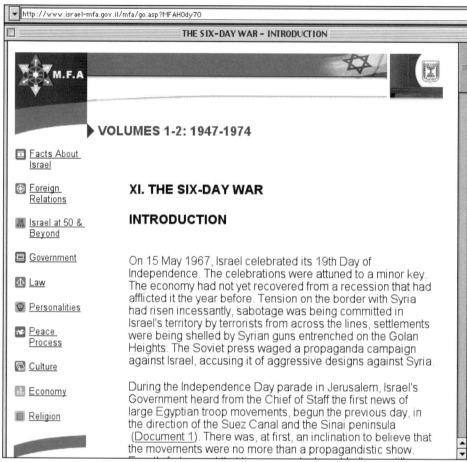

http://www.israel-mfa.gov.il/mfa/go.asp?MFAHOdy70

THE SIX-DAY WAR - INTRODUCTION

M.F.A

▶ VOLUMES 1-2: 1947-1974

- Facts About Israel
- Foreign Relations
- Israel at 50 & Beyond
- Government
- Law
- Personalities
- Peace Process
- Culture
- Economy
- Religion

XI. THE SIX-DAY WAR

INTRODUCTION

On 15 May 1967, Israel celebrated its 19th Day of Independence. The celebrations were attuned to a minor key. The economy had not yet recovered from a recession that had afflicted it the year before. Tension on the border with Syria had risen incessantly, sabotage was being committed in Israel's territory by terrorists from across the lines, settlements were being shelled by Syrian guns entrenched on the Golan Heights. The Soviet press waged a propaganda campaign against Israel, accusing it of aggressive designs against Syria.

During the Independence Day parade in Jerusalem, Israel's Government heard from the Chief of Staff the first news of large Egyptian troop movements, begun the previous day, in the direction of the Suez Canal and the Sinai peninsula (Document 1). There was, at first, an inclination to believe that the movements were no more than a propagandistic show.

FIGURE 1-56

Shavuot

CATEGORY: Food
SUBJECT: Shavuot Dishes
EXPLANATION: Locate recipes for various types of Shavuot foods, especially blintzes.

> **SITE:** Blintzes
> **URL:** ww.oldfashionedkitchen.com/golden/blintzes/blintzesnew.htm
> (see Figure 1-57, p. 142)
> **NOTES:** This commercial site features the history of blintzes, recipes, and information about foods appropriate for various Jewish holidays.

> **SITE:** Jewish Food Mailing List Archives
> **URL:** jewishfood-list.com
> **NOTES:** Click on the "Recipes" link, then on "Shavuot." Select from numerous recipes, including several kinds of blintzes and more than 40 kinds of cheesecake.

> **SITE:** Mimi's Cyber-Kitchen
> **URL:** www.cyber-kitchen.com
> **NOTES:** Click on "Mimi's Recipes," then scroll down through the recipes to select dairy dishes.

CATEGORY: Maps
SUBJECT: Israel — Ancient
EXPLANATION: Locate Jerusalem and other cities on a map of Israel. The Israelites traveled to Jerusalem to sacrifice at the Temple during Shavuot, one of the three pilgrimage festivals.

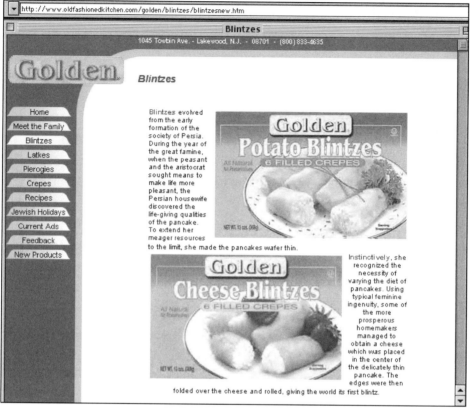

FIGURE 1-57

SITE: Bible Maps of Bible Times and Lands
URL: www.bible.ca/maps
NOTES: Choose from among several maps of ancient Israel. Note that this is a Christian site.

SITE: The Hebrews: The Major Cities and Regions
URL: www.wsu.edu/~dee/HEBREWS/ANISRMAP.HTM
NOTES: A map of the major biblical cities and regions of ancient Israel.

CATEGORY: Maps
SUBJECT: Sinai
EXPLANATION: Shavuot is the anniversary of the giving of the Torah at Mount Sinai.

> **SITE:** Egypt
> **URL:** www.lib.utexas.edu/maps/africa/egypt_pol97.jpg
> **NOTES:** A basic map of Egypt, Sinai, and Israel.

> **SITE:** Sinai.jpg
> **URL:** www.khouse.org/blueletter/images/maps/Otest/sinai.gif
> **NOTES:** A detailed map of the Sinai Peninsula.

CATEGORY: Prayers
SUBJECT: Akdamut
EXPLANATION: The *"Akdamut"* is a very special poem recited just before the Torah reading on the first day of Shavuot.

> **SITE:** Akdamut, Aramaic, and Ashkenazic Origins
> **URL:**
> www.ucalgary.ca/~elsegal/Shokel/970612_AkdamutAshkenaz.html
> **NOTES:** An explanation of the history, development, and use of the *"Akdamut"* prayer.

> **SITE:** Akdamut and Ketuvah — Shavuot at OU.ORG
> **URL:** www.ou.org/chagim/shavuot/akdamot.htm
> **NOTES:** This site contains information on the background and structure of the *"Akdamut,"* as well as an English translation.

CATEGORY: Prayers
SUBJECT: Hallel
EXPLANATION: The *Hallel*, recited during Festivals, consists of Psalms 113-118.

SITE: Hallel — "Praise of G-D" — OU.ORG

URL: www.ou.org/chagim/hallel.htm

NOTES: The site includes a detailed explanation of the development of the *Hallel* section of the *Siddur* and how and when it is recited.

CATEGORY: Ritual Objects

SUBJECT: Writing a Sefer Torah

EXPLANATION: According to tradition, Shavuot is the anniversary of the giving of the Torah at Mount Sinai. Learn how a *sofer* creates a *Sefer Torah*.

SITE: Ask the Sofer

URL: www.stam.net/AskSofer.html (see Figure 1-58, below)

NOTES: On this site, your students can e-mail questions to a *sofer*.

FIGURE 1-58

SITE: Torah

URL: www.uahcweb.org/ny/tinw/ReligiousLiving/ReligiousObjects/ Torah.htm

NOTES: This site has pictures and an explanation of how a *Sefer Torah* is written.

CATEGORY: Texts
SUBJECT: Tanach Selections
EXPLANATION: Numerous biblical passages relate to Shavuot. These include selections that mention or explore the themes of the holiday, as well as the Torah/Haftarah portions associated with the holiday (traditional and Reform). Be sure to explore: Exodus 19-20, 23:16, 34:22; Leviticus 19:9-10, 23:15-17; Numbers 28:6, 26-31; Deuteronomy 5:6-18, 8:8, 15:19-16:17, 24:19-21, 26:1-11, 31:19; Ezekiel 1:1-28, 3:12; Habakkuk 2:20-3:19; Ruth.

SITE: Divrei Torah — Commentaries

URL: shamash.org/tanach/dvar.shtml

NOTES: Scroll down for links to dozens of Torah commentary sites.

SITE: Navigating the Bible II

URL: bible.ort.org

NOTES: This site provides English and Hebrew versions of every Torah and Haftarah portion. Under "Select Language" click on "English." On the next page, the "Translation" link will provide the full text in English that can be copied and pasted into a word processing program. The "Torah" and "Haftarot" links display limited sections of the Hebrew text as graphic images. These can be copied by right-clicking on the graphic, selecting "Copy," then pasting the graphic into a word processing, page layout, or image editing document.

SITE: World Wide Study Bible
URL: www.ccel.org/wwsb
NOTES: Click on the link to the specific book of the Bible that you want, then click on the correct chapter from the list of numbers. Scroll down to "More Scriptures" and click on "Jewish Bible." Choose from among the selections. The best English selection is the link "JPS." The "Hebrew" one requires a Hebrew-reading font for your browser. All of these can be cut, pasted, and manipulated in a word processing program. Although the World Wide Study Bible is a Christian site, it has the only easily accessible online Bible text.

CATEGORY: Themes
SUBJECT: Barley
EXPLANATION: Barley is one of the seven species, the first fruit offerings of the harvest that were taken to the Temple in Jerusalem on Shavuot.

SITE: Cook's Thesaurus: Barley
URL: www.foodsubs.com/GrainBarley.html
NOTES: Information on several varieties of barley, including photos.

SITE: Digital Images 1 — Barley
URL: www.mhbgallery.com/page7.html
NOTES: Click on the thumbnail photo of a stalk of barley for a larger image.

SITE: Herbal Information Center — Barley Grass: Herbs
URL: www.kcweb.com/herb/barley.htm
NOTES: A brief article about the importance of barley and how it is used.

CATEGORY: Themes
SUBJECT: Confirmation
EXPLANATION: Learn about the ceremony of Confirmation, which takes place on Shavuot. Introduced by the Reform movement, Confirmation is now also observed by many Conservative congregations.

SITE: Reform Judaism
URL: www.rj.org
NOTES: Click on the "Ask the Rabbi" link and e-mail any questions about the ceremony of Confirmation.

SITE: United Synagogue of Conservative Judaism
URL: www.uscj.org
NOTES: Click on the link on left bottom of the menu for "Contact Us" and send an e-mail with your questions.

SITE: What Has Happened To Confirmation?
URL: www.beth-elsa.org/be_s0518.htm
NOTES: The text of a sermon explaining the history and meaning of the Confirmation ritual.

CATEGORY: Themes
SUBJECT: Conversion
EXPLANATION: The Book of Ruth is read on Shavuot. Ruth was a Moabite woman who embraced Judaism, throwing in her lot with the Jewish people. According to biblical tradition, Ruth was an ancestor of King David. Learn about conversion in each of the major branches of Judaism.

SITE: OU.org
URL: www.ou.org
NOTES: Click on the "Judaism 101" link in the left column, then on the "Do You Have a Question?" box to ask questions about Orthodox conversion.

SITE: Reform Judaism — Becoming a Jew: Questions and Answers
URL: uahc.org/outreach/becom.shtml
NOTES: Lots of information on the process and background of converting to Judaism.

SITE: United Synagogue of Conservative Judaism
URL: www.uscj.org
NOTES: Click on "Enter the Site." Then move your cursor over the "Commitment & Observance" link, and from the pop-up menu select "Marriage within the Faith," then "About Conversion in Judaism." The brief article discusses some motivations for considering conversion.

CATEGORY: Themes
SUBJECT: Figs
EXPLANATION: Figs are one of the seven species, the first fruit offerings of the harvest that were taken to the Temple in Jerusalem on Shavuot.

SITE: Fascinating Fig Facts
URL: www.valleyfig.com/funfacts.htm (see Figure 1-59, below)
NOTES: This site from a California fig growing cooperative includes a lot of information about figs, along with several pictures. For even more information, go up to the root page of the site (www.valleyfig.com) and explore some of the other links.

FIGURE 1-59

SITE: Home Fruit Production — Figs
URL: aggie-horticulture.tamu.edu/extension/homefruit/fig/fig.html
NOTES: Information about growing figs, including a listing of the various types and varieties available. Includes one photograph.

CATEGORY: Themes
SUBJECT: Honey
EXPLANATION: Honey is one of the seven species, the first fruit offerings of the harvest that were taken to the Temple in Jerusalem on Shavuot.

SITE: Capilano — From Hive To Home
URL: www.capilano.com.au/honey
NOTES: A wealth of information about honey and how it is made from an Australian honey company. Click on the "Education" link on the left, or try "Games and E-Cards" for some student activities.

SITE: Honey.com — The Honey Expert
URL: www.honey.com
NOTES: This site from the National Honey Board contains everything you might want to know about honey, including pictures. Click on the "Honey Facts" link in the left menu.

SITE: John's Beekeeping Notebook
URL: outdoorplace.org/beekeeping/index.htm
NOTES: An interesting site with lots of explanation about beekeeping and producing honey. Includes several photographs.

CATEGORY: Themes
SUBJECT: Olive Oil
EXPLANATION: The olive is one of the seven species, the first fruit offerings of the harvest that were taken to the Temple in Jerusalem on Shavuot.

SITE: Mediterranean Olive Oils and Olives
URL: www.olympia-oliveoil.com
NOTES: This is the commercial site of a Greek olive oil producer. Click on the "Olive Oil History" link on the left for information about the history of olive oil, including biblical references.

SITE: An Ode To Olives – Olive Lovers Unite
URL: www.emeraldworld.net/olive.html
NOTES: This site, created by an olive lover, features lots of information about olives, olive oil, and curing olives, plus recipes that use olives and links to places to buy books about olives.

SITE: The Olive Tree World
URL: www.olivetree.eat-online.net
NOTES: Culture, history (with pictures), literature for children, and more are found at this site devoted to olives and olive oil.

CATEGORY: Themes
SUBJECT: Pomegranates
EXPLANATION: The pomegranate is one of the seven species, the first fruit offerings of the harvest that were taken to the Temple in Jerusalem on Shavuot.

SITE: Chadmark Farms Pomegranates
URL: www.tcsn.net/chadmark/pomegranate.htm (see Figure 1-60, opposite)
NOTES: A small amount of information about pomegranates, including pictures.

SITE: Pictures of Minor Fruit Tree Species
URL: www.unifi.it/project/ueresgen29/ph.htm
NOTES: Scroll down and click on one of the links under the "Pomegranate" section for a number of views.

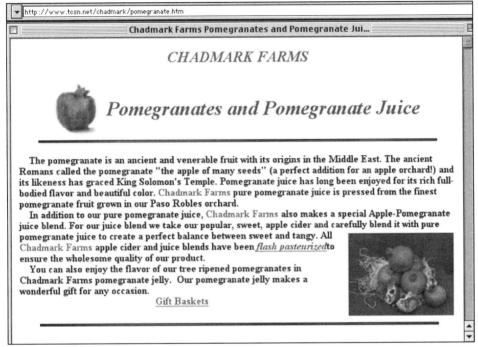

FIGURE 1-60

SITE: Pomegranate

URL: www.crfg.org/pubs/ff/pomegranate.html

NOTES: Lots of information about pomegranates. Includes a simple drawing, but no photos.

CATEGORY: Themes
SUBJECT: Grapes on the Vines
EXPLANATION: Grapes are one of the seven species, the first fruit offerings of the harvest that were taken to the Temple in Jerusalem on Shavuot.

SITE: Grapes on the Vine
URL: osu.orst.edu/food-resource/images/FRUITVEG/GRAPES/
    on_vine(ac).jpg
NOTES: A photo of bunches of grapes on the vine.

SITE: Raintree Nursery
URL: www.raintreenursery.com
NOTES: At this commercial site, pull down the "Product Index"
menu and select "Grapes." Then click any photo or link for good pictures of grapes on the vine.

CATEGORY: Themes
SUBJECT: Wheat
EXPLANATION: Wheat is one of the seven species, the first fruit offer-
ings of the harvest that were taken to the Temple in Jerusalem on
Shavuot.

SITE: Grains Nutrition Information Center
URL: www.wheatfoods.org/photos/grains.html
NOTES: Click on any of the photos for larger images of wheat and
flour. Also click on "Grains Information" in the top menu for more
background on the many uses of grains.

SITE: Photo Net — Wheat Field
URL: www.photonet-gallery.com/pnind001.htm
NOTES: A large picture of a wheat stalk.

SITE: Wheat Fields
URL: www.theslowlane.com/01tripg/palh1.html
NOTES: Photos of wheat fields and their harvest.

Tishah B'Av

CATEGORY: Arts
SUBJECT: Tishah B'Av Music
EXPLANATION: Look for music that is appropriate for Tishah B'Av, such as *"Al Naharot Bavel," "Ani Ma'amin,"* and *"Hatikvah."*

SITE: The Jewish Music Home Page
URL: www.jewishmusic.com
NOTES: In the left column, click on "Recordings," then on "Music Search." Type any of the songs above in the "Song Name:" box, then click "Submit." You will be provided with numerous links to recordings that contain a version of this song; some of them may include a link to hear the song using Real Audio.

SITE: Zemerl — The Interactive Database of Jewish Song
URL: www.princeton.edu/zemerl
NOTES: Click on the link for "Suffering" in the "Themes" category, and select from one of the choices provided. Many have midi files for listening.

CATEGORY: Historical Ties
SUBJECT: Expulsion of the Jews
EXPLANATION: Tradition teaches that Jews were expelled from both Spain and England on Tishah B'Av.

SITE: Jewish History Sourcebook: The Expulsion from Spain
URL: www.fordham.edu/halsall/jewish/1492-jews-spain1.html
NOTES: This page gives a detailed and accurate account of the expulsion of the Jews from Spain. Translated from the original Hebrew, the account was written by an Italian Jew in April or May, 1495.

SITE: Sephardim
URL: www.orthohelp.com/geneal/seph_wh2.htm#conversos
NOTES: A brief history of the events leading up to the expulsion of the Jews from Spain.

CATEGORY: Historical Ties
SUBJECT: Second Temple
EXPLANATION: Tradition teaches that the both the First and the Second Temples fell on Tishah B'Av.

SITE: Jews and Jerusalem — First Temple
URL: judaism.about.com/library/weekly/aa123100b.htm
NOTES: Information about King David, King Solomon, and the building of First Temple. Select the link to "Second Temple" for additional information.

SITE: The Temple Mount in Jerusalem
URL: www.templemount.org (see Figure 1-61, opposite)
NOTES: Links to dozens of sites concerning the location, history, and descriptions of the Temple Mount.

SITE: The Temple Mount in Jerusalem
URL: www.templemountonline.com
NOTES: Select the link for "Herod's Temple Mount in Miniature."

CATEGORY: Historical Ties
SUBJECT: Shimon Bar Kochba
EXPLANATION: Tradition says that Bar Kochba's last stand, the fortress at Betar, fell to the Romans on Tishah B'Av.

SITE: The Bar Kochba Rebellion
URL: http://www.pinn.net/~sandy/RulersCoins/BKochbaPicr.htm (see Figure 1-62, p. 156)
NOTES: A brief explanation of the Bar Kochba Revolt, including pictures of coins from that era.

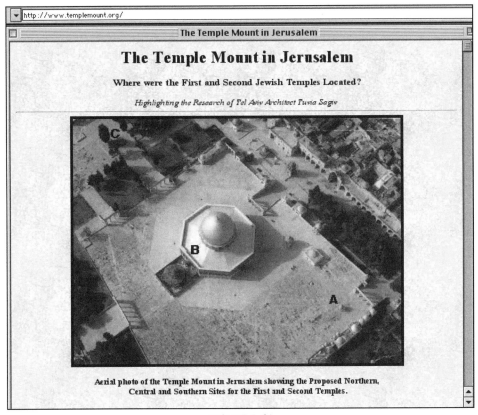

FIGURE 1-61

SITE: The Bar-Kokhba Revolt
URL: www.us-israel.org/jsource/Judaism/revolt1.html
NOTES: A lengthy article from the Jewish Virtual Library. Included are a number of additional links.

SITE: Jewish Literacy — Jewish History
URL: www.aish.com/literacy/jewishhistory/
NOTES: Scroll down quite far and click on the link, "Crash Course in Jewish History Part 37 — The Bar Kochba Revolt" for an interesting article.

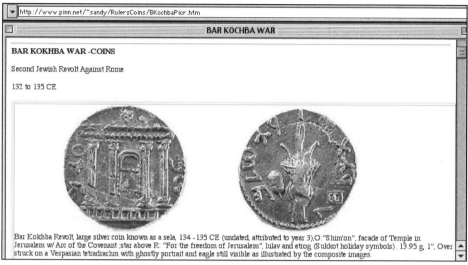

http://www.pinn.net/~sandy/RulersCoins/BKochbaPicr.htm

BAR KOCHBA WAR

BAR KOKHBA WAR -COINS

Second Jewish Revolt Against Rome

132 to 135 CE

Bar Kokhba Revolt, large silver coin known as a sela, 134 -135 CE (undated, attributed to year 3),O:"Shim'on", facade of Temple in Jerusalem w/ Arc of the Covenant ;star above R: "For the freedom of Jerusalem", lulav and etrog (Sukkot holiday symbols). 13.95 g, 1", Over struck on a Vespasian tetradrachm with ghostly portrait and eagle still visible as illustrated by the composite images.

FIGURE 1-62

CATEGORY: Personalities

SUBJECT: Yochanan Ben Zakkai

EXPLANATION: After the Second Temple was destroyed, Yochanan ben Zakkai and the Rabbis made changes in the practice of Judaism that enabled it to continue and flourish.

SITE: Yochanan ben Zakkai

URL: www.campsci.com/iguide/rebbi_yochanan_ben_zakkai.htm

NOTES: A lengthy article, with many stories about Yochanan ben Zakkai

SITE: Yochanan Ben Zakkai

URL: www.us-israel.org/jsource/biography/ben_zakkai.html

NOTES: A brief biography from the Jewish Virtual Library.

CATEGORY: Places
SUBJECT: Kotel
EXPLANATION: Tradition teaches that the both the First and the Second Temple fell on Tishah B'Av. Explore the *Kotel*, the last remnant of the Second Temple, as it looks today.

> **SITE:** Live Western Wall Camera at Aish HaTorah
> **URL:** www.aish.com/wallcam
> **NOTES:** Get a real time picture of the *Kotel*. Click "Enlarge View" for a full-screen picture.

> **SITE:** Virtual Israel Experience
> **URL:** www.us-israel.org/jsource/vie/Jerutoc.html
> **NOTES:** Pictures, information, and links to every part of Jerusalem. Select from the many links provided, both within the text and at the bottom of the page.

CATEGORY: Texts
SUBJECT: Tanach Selections
EXPLANATION: Numerous passages from the Bible deal with or relate to Tishah B'Av. These include selections that mention or explore the themes of the holiday, as well as the Torah/Haftarah portions associated with the holiday (traditional and Reform). Be sure to explore: Judges 20:26; I Samuel 7:6; Isaiah 1:1-27, 56:3; Jeremiah 1:2-28, 2:4-28, 3:4, 14:12; Jonah 3:5-8; Zechariah 8:19; Lamentations.

> **SITE:** Divrei Torah — Commentaries
> **URL:** shamash.org/tanach/dvar.shtml
> **NOTES:** Scroll down for links to dozens of Torah commentary sites.

SITE: Navigating the Bible II
URL: bible.ort.org
NOTES: This site provides English and Hebrew versions of every Torah and Haftarah portion. Under "Select Language" click on "English." On the next page, the "Translation" link will provide the full text in English that can be copied and pasted into a word processing program. The "Torah" and "Haftarot" links display limited sections of the Hebrew text as graphic images. These can be copied by right-clicking on the graphic, selecting "Copy," then pasting the graphic into a word processing, page layout, or image editing document.

SITE: World Wide Study Bible
URL: www.ccel.org/wwsb
NOTES: Click on the link to the specific book of the Bible that you want, then click on the correct chapter from the list of numbers. Scroll down to "More Scriptures" and click on "Jewish Bible." Choose from among the selections. The best English selection is the link "JPS." The "Hebrew" one requires a Hebrew-reading font for your browser. All of these can be cut, pasted, and manipulated in a word processing program. Although the World Wide Study Bible is a Christian site, it has the only easily accessible online Bible text.

CATEGORY: Themes
SUBJECT: Anti-Semitism
EXPLANATION: Fighting anti-Semitism is a key element in preventing persecution of Jews in the future.

SITE: ADL: Fighting Anti-Semitism, Bigotry, and Extremism
URL: www.adl.org
NOTES: This is the web site for the Anti-Defamation League. It includes news and resources on such topics as anti-Semitism, terrorism, religious freedom, civil rights, extremism, and the Holocaust. Explore the many links on the left side and bottom of the main page.

SITE: The Jewish Links Directory — Anti-Semitism and the Holocaust
URL: members.tripod.com/~jewish_links/JEWS/anti.html
NOTES: Select from over 200 links that deal with some aspect of anti-Semitism.

CATEGORY: Themes
SUBJECT: Holocaust
EXPLANATION: The horrors of the Holocaust are often connected to Tishah B'Av.

SITE: Remember.org
URL: www.remember.org
NOTES: Lots of graphics, information, and links to information about the Holocaust.

SITE: Teachers Guide To the Holocaust
URL: fcit.usf.edu/holocaust
NOTES: This outstanding site provides a comprehensive overview of the people and events of the Holocaust.

SITE: The United States Holocaust Museum
URL: www.ushmm.org (see Figure 1-63, p. 160)
NOTES: This is the official web site for the museum. Much of the collection and information about the museum is accessible.

CATEGORY: Themes
SUBJECT: Mourning
EXPLANATION: The customs of mourning govern the observance of Tishah B'Av.

SITE: Guide To the Jewish Funeral
URL: www.jewish-funerals.org/brochure.htm
NOTES: Information about all aspects of the Jewish funeral and Jewish burial practices.

FIGURE 1-63

SITE: Jewish Death and Mourning Customs
URL: www.utah.edu/hillel/mourning.htm
NOTES: A lengthy, easy to read article that covers all aspects of Jewish death and mourning customs. It is also available to download in PDF format.

Rosh Chodesh

CATEGORY: Arts
SUBJECT: Rosh Chodesh Music
EXPLANATION: Listen to songs with a Rosh Chodesh theme, such as "Rosh Chodesh Moon" from the album *A Moon Note* by Miraj, "Rosh Chodesh" from the album *The Length of Our Days*, by Marsha Rose Attie, and "Birkat Halevana" from the album *Live at Carnegie Hall* by Debbie Friedman.

> **SITE:** The Jewish Music Home Page
> **URL:** www.jewishmusic.com (see Figure 1-64, p. 160)
> **NOTES:** Select "All" from the "Search:" box, then type any of the songs above, or the term "Rosh Chodesh," in the "For:" box. Alternatively, click on "Recordings" in the left menu, then select "Music Search." Then type "Rosh Chodesh" in the "Keyword:" box and click "Submit." You will be provided with several links to recordings, some of which may include sound clips of Rosh Chodesh songs.

> **SITE:** Sounds Write Productions Inc.
> **URL:** www.soundswrite.com
> **NOTES:** Click on the "Search Sounds Write" box, then type "Rosh Chodesh" and click "Search." Follow the links to appropriate albums and songs. The alternate spelling "Rosh Hodesh" yields different results.

CATEGORY: Maps
SUBJECT: Jerusalem — Ancient
EXPLANATION: In ancient times, signal fires were lit on the hilltops around Jerusalem to proclaim the beginning of the new month.

FIGURE 1-64

SITE: Jerusalem in Old Maps and Views
URL: www.israel.org/mfa/go.asp?MFAH00jb0
NOTES: Explore this site to select maps and information about the history of Jerusalem.

SITE: Sites
URL: www1.huji.ac.il/njeru/sites.htm
NOTES: Pictures, information, and a map of archeological sites in Jerusalem's history.

CATEGORY: Prayers
SUBJECT: Hallel
EXPLANATION: The *Hallel*, recited on Rosh Chodesh, consists of Psalms 113-118.

SITE: Hallel — "Praise of G-D" — OU.ORG
URL: www.ou.org/chagim/hallel.htm
NOTES: The site includes a detailed explanation of the development of the *Hallel* section of the *Siddur* and how and when it is recited.

CATEGORY: Ritual Objects
SUBJECT: Shofar
EXPLANATION: The *shofar* is sounded to proclaim the beginning of the new month.

SITE: Judaica Online Shofars
URL: www.judaicaonline.com/CT_Misc/PRMS2_MSG427.htm
NOTES: A number of pictures of *shofarot* are provided on this commercial site.

SITE: Shofar
URL: www.uahcweb.org/ny/tinw/ReligiousLiving/ReligiousObjects/
    Shofar.htm
NOTES: This site contains numerous pictures and explanations, as well as the blessings connected with blowing the *shofar*. Also included are links to wav files to listen to the *shofar*.

CATEGORY: Texts
SUBJECT: Tanach Selections
EXPLANATION: There are several biblical passages that relate to Rosh Chodesh, including selections that mention or explain the themes of the holiday. Be sure to explore: Numbers 10:10, 28:11-15; I Samuel 20:18-42; II Kings 4:8-37; Amos 8:5; Isaiah 1:13-14.

SITE: Divrei Torah — Commentaries
URL: shamash.org/tanach/dvar.shtml
NOTES: Scroll down for links to dozens of Torah commentary sites.

SITE: Navigating the Bible II
URL: bible.ort.org
NOTES: This site provides English and Hebrew versions of every Torah and Haftarah portion. Under "Select Language" click on "English." On the next page, the "Translation" link will provide the full text in English that can be copied and pasted into a word processing program. The "Torah" and "Haftarot" links display limited sections of the Hebrew text as graphic images. These can be copied by right-clicking on the graphic, selecting "Copy," then pasting the graphic into a word processing, page layout, or image editing document.

SITE: World Wide Study Bible
URL: www.ccel.org/wwsb
NOTES: Click on the link to the specific book of the Bible that you want, then click on the correct chapter from the list of numbers. Scroll down to "More Scriptures" and click on "Jewish Bible." Choose from among the selections. The best English selection is the link "JPS." The "Hebrew" one requires a Hebrew-reading font for your browser. All of these can be cut, pasted, and manipulated in a word processing program. Although the World Wide Study Bible is a Christian site, it has the only easily accessible online Bible text.

CATEGORY: Themes
SUBJECT: Calendar
EXPLANATION: The Jewish calendar is primarily based on the phases of the moon. It differs from the secular calendar, which is based on the cycles of the sun. Rosh Chodesh is the celebration of the New moon each month.

SITE: 5763 — The Jewish Calendar Year (2002 – 2003)
URL: www.ou.org/calendar/5763/default.htm
NOTES: A listing of all of the Jewish holidays for the next year, including work restrictions and other important notes. To update this calendar in subsequent years, simply change the year in the URL (e.g., "5769" rather than "5768").

SITE: Hebrew Calendar Science and Myths
URL: www.geocities.com/Athens/1584
NOTES: All sorts of interesting information about the Jewish calendar, its development, accuracy, and more.

SITE: Jewish Calendar
URL: www.uscj.org/midwest/milwaukeecbi/jr_jewis.htm
NOTES: This site contains an explanation of how the Jewish calendar is organized.

CATEGORY: Themes
SUBJECT: Phases of the Moon
EXPLANATION: Explore pictures of the various phases of the moon.

SITE: Earth and Moon Viewer
URL: www.fourmilab.ch/earthview/vplanet.html
NOTES: Lots of pictures, information, and links to material about the moon.

SITE: The Moon
URL: www.netaxs.com/~mhmyers/moon.tn.html
NOTES: Numerous photographs of the various phases of the moon.

SITE: The Moon
URL: seds.lpl.arizona.edu/nineplanets/nineplanets/luna.html (see Figure 1-65, p. 166)
NOTES: A great overview of the moon, with several photos and many links to additional moon sites.

FIGURE 1-65

SITE: Virtual Reality Moon Phases Pictures

URL: tycho.usno.navy.mil/vphase.html

NOTES: View images of the phases of the moon for any date in modern history.

Conclusion

This book has provided you with countless Internet resources related to Jewish holidays. Just imagine the potential for your students! For a unit on Shabbat, your students can easily find recipes for *cholent* and other special Shabbat foods. At Simchat Torah, you can explore in detail the process a *sofer* follows in writing a *Sefer Torah*. At Pesach, you can enliven your school's model *Seder* by including sections of Uncle Eli's Special-for-Kids Most Fun Ever Under-the-Table Passover Haggadah, written in the style of Dr. Seuss. To observe Yom HaShoah, your class can take a virtual tour of the United States Holocaust Museum in Washington, D.C., or Yad Vashem in Jerusalem.

This is not a fantasy, nor is it Jewish science fiction. This is the reality available to you now, thanks to the limitless resources of what can be called "The Ultimate Jewish Teacher Resource Center" — the Internet. Using the information provided in this book, your Jewish holiday curriculum can be greatly enhanced with interesting, relevant material that was previously inaccessible and is now available to you with just a few clicks of your mouse. You and your curriculum are now "Wired into Teaching Jewish Holidays." Enjoy the journey!

APPENDIX A
Glossary of Terms

address   The location of a site on the Internet, usually
                       beginning with "http://www." or just www.
                       (sometimes they begin with numbers); also
                       referred to as the URL of the site

bookmark   A favorite site that you place in a special menu
                       on your browser, thereby enabling you to link
                       instantaneously to that site simply by clicking on
                       the name. In Netscape Navigator these are called
                       "Bookmarks"; in Microsoft Internet Explorer, they
                       are called "Favorites."

browser   The software that allows you to view sites on the
                       Internet

cyberspace/   The world of the Internet and online services
cyberworld

directory   A site that lists other Internet sites by category,
                       similar in function to a search engine

e-mail   Mail messages sent electronically from one com-
                       puter to another; an e-mail address contains the
                       person's user name, the "@" sign, and then the
                       domain name

font
The style and size of type for the text on your computer screen and on your printout

GIF
One type of graphic file that is used on Internet sites

graphic
The term for drawings, pictures, or artistic word designs that are used on the Internet

home page
An Internet site dedicated to a topic or a personal interest; home pages are the format that individuals and businesses use to promote their interests on the Internet

Internet
The overall term used to describe the global system of networked computers which allow the transfer of information and communication between users; in this book, it also refers to all online services: the World Wide Web, telnet, news groups, and e-mail services and systems

JPG or JPEG
Another type of graphic file used on Internet sites, usually for photographs

key word
A primary word used for a subject search at a web site; also referred to as "search term." (To users of America Online, a "key word" takes you to a specific content area of the AOL site.)

link
Words, phrases, or graphics that when "clicked on," or "selected," provide a direct connection to another Internet site

meta-search
Conducting a search for content on the Internet using a search engine that searches other search engines and displays a range of results

online   Being connected to the Internet through a per-
                            sonal computer

root page   The foundation page of a particular web site, to
                            which all other pages of that site are linked.
                            Generally, this is the first part of the URL, ending
                            in ".com," ".org," ".gov," etc.

search engine   A "directory assistance" for the Internet which
                            allows a user to locate sites whose titles or
                            descriptions contain specific search words

site   Another name for a home page location on the
                            Internet

URL   Short for "Universal Resource Locator"; also
                            known as an address; the official location of a
                            site on the Internet

web site/   Another name for a home page — the information
web page   someone or some company places at a particular
                            URL

World Wide Web   For all practical purposes, another name for the
                            Internet

APPENDIX B
How to "Bookmark" a Web Site

Your web browser software allows you to save the address of a specific web page so that you can revisit it quickly and easily, without having to type in the complete address each time. In Microsoft Internet Explorer, these saved pages are called "Favorites;" in Netscape Navigator or Communicator, they are known as "Bookmarks." When you come across a site that you find valuable and may wish to view again, follow the instructions below for adding that site to your list of Favorites or Bookmarks.

In Microsoft Internet Explorer:
1. While online, go to the page you want to add to your Favorites list.
2. On the **Favorites** menu, click **Add to Favorites**.
3. You can accept the name of the site as shown, or type a new name for the page if you wish, something that will make sense to you in the future.

To open one of your favorite pages, click the **Favorites** menu, and from the drop-down menu, click the page you wish to open.

In Netscape Navigator or Communicator:
4. While online, go to the web page you want to bookmark.
5. Click **Bookmarks** (on a Macintosh, open the Bookmarks menu by clicking on the green bookmark icon to the right of the Go menu).
6. Choose **Add Bookmark**.

To revisit a bookmarked web page, click **Bookmarks** on the toolbar and choose a bookmarked page from the dropdown menu. (On a Macintosh, open the **Bookmarks** menu by clicking on the green bookmark icon.)